DISCOVER YOUR INNER GPS

Praise for
'Discover your inner GPS'

"The title is very appropriate as it is a map for inner well-being and development of the self. Karen's extensive studies in various fields such as counselling and acupuncture, makes her the ideal person to lay out a map for those seeking fulfilment. The book is set out in various steps to be followed and worked at to develop a healthy and holistic lifestyle.

For myself as a GP who always had an interest in holistic medicine and used acupuncture and hypnosis when needed. I would greatly have appreciated having a book like this to map my way in the early days. I can strongly recommend it for anyone seeking the right path."

Dr. Frank McKenna, General Practitioner

"This is such an important book, one that I feel everyone should read at some point in their lives.

Karen provides insights and understanding and an abundance of tools to assist you with getting your life back on track. You'll be surprised at how quickly these techniques will have you enjoying life again.

You will find a happiness, peace and contentment that just seeps into every fibre of your being. It creates a sort of domino affect shifting your way of thinking and your perception and outlook from within and reflecting outwards on all your life's experiences moving forwards.

A truly positive and uplifting book "

Mary Butler, Aer Lingus

"An extraordinary journey through Karen's life. How, with a little help, she discovered her voice, banished her demons, and in the process created a valuable blueprint for living. A book that reveals, in easy to follow steps, how it's possible to analyse your life and relationships... and how minor adjustments to the way you perceive yourself and others will have life changing consequences. This is a book everyone must read!"

Colm Roe, Director M. Roe & Sons

I loved Karen O'Donnell's book "Discover Your innerGPS", and the way she used her own life story to captivate me as a reader – so much so that I read it first in one full day and night session – and have since gone back to re-read sections of it several times. For me it was opportune as I was going through a difficult divorce and change in my life. Karen's book, "Discover Your Inner GPS", helped me discover my "innerGPS" and navigate my way to a new start in life.
Even her Contents page is a vivid reminder to me, as a lifelong sailor, of the importance of waypoints, not only in maritime navigation, but also on the voyage of life! The book fleshes out the contents in an extraordinarily simple and understandable narrative and recommendations for self-improvement. I cannot recommend it strongly enough!

Brendan Haughton, Sales Director

"What an inciteful read. Karen cleverly uses her own wake-up call to wake us up. Her example makes you re-examine your true goals and the straightforward tools help you achieve them. A recommended read if you're harbouring a true goal but not sure how to get there"

Bob Ferguson
CEO of Bob Ferguson Communications Ltd.

If you have ever felt" Invisible" or weighed down with life, this book is a must read. Discovering your Inner GPS is an inspiring and practical approach to ridding you of your self-doubt and negativity, allowing you to discover the way home to your real self and your true purpose in life. Filled with personal stories, Karen takes you on a real-life journey which provides the inspiration and the tools to help you make a difference in the world. A must read.

Gerry French,
Cartographer @ Geological Survey of Ireland

DISCOVER YOUR INNER GPS

Your Navigation system for success, mental clarity and happiness.

KAREN O'DONNELL

YouCaxton Publications

Oxford & Shrewsbury

ISBN 978-1-912419-90-6
Printed and bound in Great Britain.

Published by YouCaxton Publications 2019
YCBN: 01

YouCaxton Publications

enquiries@youcaxton.co.uk

Dedicated to my parachutes in life

My mum Carmel,

my husband Fran

& my children -

Luca, Callum & Sadhbh

Contents

Part III — Explore Courageously

Introduction

I realised after many years of formal education that I had lot to learn about life. I dipped my toe into the practice of positive thinking towards the end of my teenage years, though it wasn't until my mid thirties that I realised I needed to go far deeper than I had been going. To delve down way below the surface and embrace all the lessons my life had to offer.

In 2006, I suffered what can only be described as a near-death experience. (Indeed, I did die!) And as you might imagine, this served as an effective wakeup call! I thought that I had dealt with or 'processed' my early life traumas. However, my sabbatical with 'death' revealed I needed to *go deep* and clear out the emotional scars of these early events.

I wrote this book to show that you don't have to wait until some life-altering event forces you to 'wake up'. You can take charge *now* and make the changes you need on your terms. You can avoid the roadblocks, dead-ends and unnecessary detours. You can be in the driving seat of your story and reach the destination you want.

Have you ever asked yourself...?
Why am I unhappy?
Why don't I get the success I deserve?
Why do I have difficulty with relationships?
Why do bad things keep happening to me?

Have you ever wondered...?
Is there more to life than this?
Why am I here?
What is my real purpose?
Why does life seem to be passing me by?

If you have ever had any of these questions, then *this book for you!*

After many years of self-discovery, and a dedication to acquiring and training with a variety of therapies and modalities, I developed a powerful program of self-discovery. My *innerGPS* system is a program of self-enquiry, mental and emotional support, and dynamic techniques and strategies designed to help you find the real you and experience life as you are meant to live it — with happiness, prosperity and optimism.

This program has taken many years to develop and includes numerous incredibly powerful strategies, tools and techniques, some of which I share with you in this book. Over almost two decades of working with clients, one-to-one and in group settings, I have condensed and gathered my most effective strategies and practical steps to assist you in navigating your way to your desired destination. I also teach this as a workshop series helping you create change through practical steps that alter how you view life.

The purpose of this book is to create a simple and effective guide to personal transformation that will help you understand how you can change your life to the one you desire and deserve. When you apply these strategies and techniques to your everyday, you can then truly own your own life.

Embrace and complete all the many exercises that I share with you in this book and experience the results for yourself. When you boldly explore your inner world, uncover your sabotaging primitive roadmap and discover your true *innerGPS*, you too can live the life you're supposed to be living. The one you have dreamed about, or the one you suspect is out here waiting for you, even if you don't know what that looks like yet.

I share with you the outline of my own primitive roadmap and my journey to discovering my *innerGPS*. The information and techniques will lift and guide you in moving out of your own shadow, empowering you to step into your true greatness.

All I ask is that you step off the cliff edge and *go deep,* making sure you have this *parachute* strapped securely to your back, and transform your life with the help of the step-by-step exercises and *strategies* I have outlined in this book. That's how you will learn to navigate your way to success and happiness with your i*nnerGPS!*

PART I

THE MAP THAT GOT YOU HERE WON'T GET YOU THERE

Chapter 1

A Life-or-Death Situation... Literally!

"Life is very, very simple and easy to understand, but we complicate it with the beliefs and ideas that we create."

Don Miguel Ruiz

"Clear!"... pufh
4 August 2006, 2:45pm

Dr. Froese, with the aid of a defibrillator, tried shocking me back to life. A young doctor placed an artificial respiration device over my mouth and began squeezing air back into my lifeless body. Dr. Froese resumed the chest compressions he'd begun a few minutes earlier and administered adrenaline and atropine. Hospital staff continued working relentlessly as they tried frantically to save me.

Earlier that day, Friday, 4 August 2006, I attended the maternity hospital with my husband to give birth to my second child. The excitement of finally meeting him was huge. Callum was born by caesarean section at 1.45pm. After the birth, Callum was taken away to be cleaned up and my obstetrician completed the operation before my transfer to the recovery ward. My husband, Fran, joined me straight away and I got to hold my new baby boy for the first time. We were surrounded by a couple of nurses and three other new mums, who were basking in the pure thrill of holding their new bundles of joy. I thought they were all in the same situation as me. Then, at 2:30pm, still in the recovery ward, I began to feel a slight unease. Something was happening. Whatever it was, it was happening quickly. A sense of deep foreboding came over me. I turned to my husband Fran and said, "Look after Callum, I can't breathe!" I felt a choking sensation and life draining from me. I vomited, gasped one final time and stopped breathing.

Life hung in the balance.

The strangest feeling engulfed me. I became aware of an unusual perspective. I couldn't *feel* myself. I just had an *awareness* of what was going on around me. And I could see myself. I was watching everything take place before me, like I was a spectator in the room watching from an almost elevated viewpoint. As the scene unfolded, I felt quite detached as I observed all the commotion with the dawning realisation of what was happening.

Hospital staff hurriedly wheeled the three mothers with their newborn babies out of our communal recovery room, as they looked on horrified.

As this was taking place around me, I noticed something strange. I could also see past events from my life. Time slowed as each different scene played out. There was a common theme to the scenes I saw: me being invisible. In this first scene, I was hiding in my bedroom wardrobe, hiding behind the hanging clothes, hiding from my drunken father, who wanted to teach me a lesson. My childhood cheekiness was frowned upon by my father. He was very much of the opinion that children should be "seen and not heard". Fuelled with a belly full of brandy, he would 'hunt me down' if I'd spoken up or 'answered back' in his eye, earlier that day. If he caught me, he would beat me violently. These assaults were always carried out when the rest of the family were out of the house. I was the youngest of four children so I suppose I was an easy target. Life as a young child was an anxious time for me. I'd walk on eggshells during the day and hide in the evenings until my father fell asleep and it was safe to come out.

"Clear!"... pufh
4 August 2006, 2:50pm

Dr. Froese shocked me for the second time. He looked towards the monitor. No change. He shouted instructions to the attentive staff as he again resumed chest compressions. The young doctor tirelessly squeezed air into my lungs, focusing completely on his task. My life was literally in their hands and they put every ounce of energy into it.

From my unique viewpoint, life scenes continued to divert my attention. Although this time, the event I could see did not recall any physical pain, it did remind me of an emotional pain. Its importance lies mostly in that it validated my sense of being treated as 'invisible'. The scene was from a time just after I had made my first Holy Communion. Armed with the gifts of money I had received on making my Holy Communion, I was taken into Dublin city by an aunt to do some shopping. My aunt dropped me off at Woolworths in Henry Street so I could spend some of my money. She told me to do my shopping and then to wait in the window and she would be back for me in 20 minutes. I went and bought some chocolate to share with my brother and sisters and I also bought tiny yellow sticky alphabet letters for sticking on stationary and making cards. I happily skipped around the shop, and when I was finished, I waited in the shop window. Woolworths had big floor-to-ceiling glass windows and large window ledge where you could sit. I sat and waited for my aunt's return. I waited and waited. I waited for hours. I became hungry. I even ate the chocolate I'd bought for my sisters and brother, I was so hungry. It was several hours later when my mother came rushing into the shop. My aunt had forgotten where she'd left me and gone home without me! Although I was sitting in one of the largest windows in Henry Street, I wasn't seen by my aunt as she looked. I was invisible.

"Clear!"... pufh
4 August 2006, 2:53pm

Dr. Froese shocked me for the third time. He looked to the young doctor who kept squeezing his artificial respiration device. Dr. Froese continued relentlessly with chest compressions and the diligent young doctor, whose hands were aching from the relentless squeezing, continued to breathe for me, like his life depended on it. Even though it was my life that depended on it.

From my vantage point, another past scene came to my awareness. This scene was from a time during my teenage years. I seemed to be on the periphery of my own life, not quite centre stage, in fact almost in the background. Everyone in this scene appeared in vibrant colours, whereas I seemed sepia. At this stage of life, I was not playing the part of me, but wearing a mask or several masks, being different versions of myself. Why would I do this? To be accepted by my peers, my friends, I hid my true self, the real me behind a mask. I'd made myself invisible.

Having witnessed these early scenes from my life, I realised that the earlier childhood experiences created strategies to cope in situations. These strategies were like a roadmap that was helping me navigate life. However, this roadmap was based on the experiences of a young girl. Part of my roadmap was built on the belief that 'it's not safe being me'. For instance, speaking up for myself got me into trouble; over time, therefore, I learned to be quiet. By disappearing in plain sight, I would keep myself safe from harm. I would be a muted and invisible version of myself. For me, being 'invisible' kept me out of trouble with my Dad. And I stayed invisible. I was the sister, the daughter, the wife, the mother. *But where was I?*

What was my identity? I seemed to doubt myself, constantly questioning what I was doing.

As I revisited these scenes looking down on myself, I felt like I had two sides. One side that had been conditioned to be invisible, an invisibility that *kept me safe*; and the other side, my true self, that simply wanted to be seen and be heard.

How many times do we compromise our *true self*, in order to be accepted by others? How often do we place restrictions on ourselves so that we are more acceptable to others? How many times had I shied away from opportunities or experiences because I just didn't want to take a chance? Yet deep within, a part of me was screaming out to do just that. *Be seen! Be heard!* As my life hung in the balance, the voice of each side argued for their existence. Both voices gave convincing arguments as to why I should take their direction!

My invisibility was urging me to dissolve and have no more life struggles; My True Self urged me to stand up for myself and keep living. I was watching this all take place, as my window of vision became increasingly small and I became increasingly what I had been working towards unconsciously all my life... *invisible*.

The scenes flashed. You could say my world flashed before my eyes, but it wasn't my whole life. The images had a strong theme, me being invisible; me as a teenager, not being seen; me in the window waiting for my aunt, not being seen; me hiding in my wardrobe, behind the hanging clothes, hiding from my father, not being seen. Phrases jumped in front of me... seen and not heard, seen and not heard.

4 August 2006, 3:01pm

Twenty-six minutes after I first stopped breathing, I saw Dr. Froese quietly instruct the staff to discontinue their efforts. The young doctor stopped squeezing air into my lungs. Nurses backed away from the bed and took note of the time. The commotion settled down and one doctor sat in a nearby chair. My vitals were checked, as the nurse approached my husband.

Earlier, I had welcomed our son Callum into this world. Now, as I looked around the room, my husband Fran and our new baby son were towards the back of the recovery room. I saw the nurse approach Fran, as she put her hand on his shoulder and in a whisper said, "Sorry, she's gone". Fran glanced over at our son in his cot and buried his head in his hands.

I was slipping away. Somewhere deep inside me came a screaming whisper, an inner knowing.

'Be seen! Be heard!'

I had a split second to choose my fate. Be invisible and slip away, or be seen, be heard, and return.

Beep, beep, beep...

The heart monitor jumped into action to announce my return! There was a flurry of activity as doctors responded to my new status.

3 August 2006

Let me take you back twenty-four hours to Thursday, 3rd August when I attended my obstetrician for an internal examination to see if I was favourable for a 'normal' delivery. With my first son Luca, the birth had started out normal enough. However, he had got stuck and an emergency caesarean section had been the best option for us both. For my second pregnancy, I was keen on having a vaginal birth. Hugh O'Connor, my consultant, was a fantastic obstetrician — caring, down to earth, with a lovely manner about him. I felt so safe in his care. While Hugh carried out this internal examination, I suddenly felt an excruciating pain. I have a high pain threshold, but I screamed out and almost leapt from the bed. Well, as much as a heavily pregnant woman can leap! I was a little disappointed to learn that this birth would again be by caesarean section. Hugh was flying out the following day to Portugal for the August Bank Holiday weekend. We said our goodbyes and scheduled the delivery for the following week.

After the examination, my mum drove me and my son Luca home while Fran stayed in Dublin with work. It was a beautiful day as we travelled back to Co. Wicklow. I was super excited. In just a week, we would meet our little boy. Yes, we knew our baby was a *him*. When I was pregnant with Luca, I had wanted to know the gender of my baby then too, though Fran had been happy to wait. We'd been calling our child 'It', and I wanted to change that. When attending the maternity hospital for a regular check-up, I turned to Fran and said, "I respect your wishes for not wanting to know what sex our baby is, but I would like to know. Why don't we just get the nurse to tell me and you can wait another 20 weeks before you find out?" Fran thought about it for a nanosecond, and replied, "I want to know now. Let's find out!"

So, there I was, knowing we were just a week away from meeting Callum. We had moved from Celbridge, Co. Kildare to Tinahely, Co. Wicklow the previous year. Although I loved living in the countryside, I was further away from my family and friends. When we lived in Celbridge, my mam and I would regularly meet on Saturday mornings and go to Dublin city. We didn't need a reason to meet up. Most of the time we'd just hang out and go around the shops and have breakfast. I loved those times so much. As she was driving me and Luca back home, we chatted busily about the coming week and what I had left to do. My bag was already packed. In fact, I must have repacked it 20 times! Seeing those tiny baby outfits and visualising Callum in them had made me reorganise the bag over and over. Spending the next couple of days with Mam was going to be great. We got Luca off to bed and sat around chatting about anything and everything. I always loved hearing stories of her own mother, my Nana Josie; another remarkable woman who was known for making the most amazing brown bread. Nana Josie was so kind and so funny, with a lot of wisdom thrown in too. Mam had been so close to her and her passing left a big hole in my mam's heart. At 10pm, I went to bed exhausted from the day and an evening of chit-chat.

I awoke the next morning at about 7am to the sun beaming in through the window and the discomfort of a soaking wet bed! It took me a couple of moments to realise what was going on. *So, this is what happens when your waters break*, I thought. My mam is quite a calm person, generally. However, a two-hour drive to the Coombe Hospital with me was not what she had bargained for that morning. I phoned Fran excitedly with the news and then called ahead to the hospital. Hugh could perform the delivery that day, but needed to leave the hospital by 2pm to catch his flight to Portugal. I really wanted him to perform the caesarean section as he is such a wonderful surgeon. We were against the clock. In the excitement, I almost forgot the 20-times-packed pregnancy bag! We gathered what we needed, packed a bag for Luca and bundled into the car.

It was an interesting drive to hospital. My mother, who rarely swears, doesn't speed, and is usually very calm, was now in a situation she was not expecting. Picture the scene, my mam in the driving seat with a flustered me beside her. Colourful language was used by the both of us, mostly directed towards other drivers on the road. Suffice to say, speed limits were ignored and mam got me to Dublin on time. I met Fran at his mother's house and we made our way together to the hospital, thankfully in time to have Hugh deliver our baby. It was not the type of birth I wanted, but I was just so excited to meet our little boy at last. The delivery of my son Callum seemed to go perfectly. Until the recovery room, when I turned to Fran and said, "Look after Callum"...

My complication was quite rare. I had suffered an amniotic fluid embolism. This occurs when amniotic fluid enters the bloodstream, resulting in a massive heart attack. While the likelihood of an amniotic fluid embolism occurring is rare, recovery is even rarer. I had stopped breathing for 26 minutes. I had had no pulse for 26 minutes. My heart had stopped beating for 26 minutes. I was dead for 26 minutes. The prognosis for recovery was not good!

When my heart monitor beeped back into action, I was intubated and immediately transferred from the Coombe Maternity Hospital to the intensive care unit at St. James's Hospital. For the first few hours in St. James's Hospital, I underwent tests, x-rays and had what's called a greenfield filter inserted. This is an inferior vena cava filter, a small metal device that traps large clot fragments and prevents them from travelling through the vena cava to the heart and lungs. This was positioned just below my heart and breaks down any potential clots that might otherwise enter my heart. This little device although generally used as a temporary measure is still in me. I had no idea of its existence until I had an unrelated scan in 2013. A cannula was also inserted in my chest area so that medication could be administered directly to my heart, if required. My body was recovering from a traumatic event and I was heavily medicated to allow my body heal. I have a hazy memory of events over the following few days.

5 August 2006

I was extubated and totally disorientated with no memory of the previous day. In fact, any memory of my life and those people dear to me was severely impaired. I didn't know why I was in the hospital. My chest felt like it had been flattened by a truck, from the CPR work at the Coombe Hospital. I didn't know what month it was. *I didn't know who I was!* On the morning after my son was born, I had stroke-like symptoms with limited movement down the left side of my body. What kept going through my head were my early childhood memories, those scenes where I was invisible, and the frustration and anger that I now couldn't talk! There was nothing more frustrating than having this going over and over in your head — Be Seen! Be Heard! — yet being unable to speak! It was the one clear thought I was having, yet I couldn't action it. I am not known for being a patient person and I was not a patient patient on this day. I just wanted out of this unfamiliar situation. I just wanted to be home.

6 August 2006

Still confined to my hospital bed, my speech was slurred and slow, probably as a result of my brain being without oxygen for so long. People couldn't understand me, which I found hugely frustrating, and my lovely nurse kept asking me questions, questions that I felt were both stupid and annoying. Questions about what day it was. Questions about where I was. Questions about how many children I had. I knew I was in hospital and that this lady was my nurse, though I gave inaccurate answers. I was in a Dublin hospital, but thought I was in Kilkenny. I didn't know that I had just given birth to my second child. In fact, I thought I had four children. I knew my date of birth, but nothing of the birth of my new baby, nor the name of my three-year-old son. I was not making any sense, yet of course, I was convinced I was being accurate and they were all idiots! I couldn't piece together what was happening to me. I kept attempting to get out of the bed, much to the shock of the nurses. I was allowed to sit in a chair, and although I received repeated instructions not to stand, I ignored them all and kept trying to get up. I just wanted to get home.

I did not recognise pictures of my son Luca, or any member of my family. Fran was with me almost constantly for the first 48 hours, and while I recognised him, I didn't know his name. It was all very confusing. I recall wincing with pain when I moved. I was unable to explain where the pain was located. The nurse would go through a variety of body parts that may be feeling pain, but I couldn't answer. I was unaware of the large caesarean section incision, which the nurses attended to. During these first few days, I would tire quickly and slept a lot.

Initially, Callum was kept in the special care baby unit in the maternity hospital, but after the first few days, my sister Sharon took over his care and brought him home. Her own daughter Caoileann was just four months old. Of course, in my state, I had no idea this was taking place. There were so many people taking care of me, my needs and the needs of my family. And my response was almost *indifference*. I know that I was 'not in my right mind' at the time, but it wasn't the first time, nor probably the last, that I would take someone's help for granted. People have been there for me, lifting me up, being a *parachute* for me, and at times, I have taken that lifeline for granted...

7 August 2006

It was three days after Callum's birth that my speech became somewhat clearer. The nurses could understand my ramblings. Those unfortunate, amazing women! They could understand that I wanted to get out of the bed and go to the bathroom on my own. I just couldn't understand why I was not allowed. The nurses wanted me to rest. Why? Why would I need rest? Once I realised I had a child, I became quite agitated that I couldn't go. Fran and Mam were asked to leave and let me rest.

Now that I was finding my voice, I kept talking to the nurses. I was speaking out, though hearing a confused person speaking garbage must have been difficult for the hospital staff. I look back at my time in St. James's Hospital and realise what absolute angels nurses are. Not only did they care for my medical needs, but they tolerated my confusion. No doubt I was a challenging patient.

By the end of the day, I had made enough progress and constant insistence that I was allowed to go to the bathroom unaided, though the nurse accompanied me. This was progress. This was me getting my independence back. This was me becoming stronger.

I still couldn't retain the knowledge that I had just given birth to beautiful Callum a few days before. When the nurse, for the umpteenth time, would tell me that I had just had a baby boy, I sobbed. I would express breast milk and Fran would take it to my son. Every time I was told about Callum, I wanted to get to him and couldn't understand why I was being kept from him.

8 August 2006

Four days after Callum's birth, I was finally moved from intensive care into a general women's ward of six women. I was quite alert, though remained confused. I just couldn't hold onto the fact that I was in hospital, why I was there or that I had a new son. The wound across my abdomen was so painful, and I continued to bring this to the attention of the nursing staff and doctors, even though I did not want to take any painkillers nor did I realise it was from my caesarean section. Somewhere in the recesses of my mind was the memory of the birth of my first child, Luca. When he had been born, I'd had a morphine pump to help with the pain from that caesarean section. When I used it, though, I felt drowsy. So drowsy that one time, I was holding him and almost dropped him on the bed while feeding. The sheer fright of that incident stayed with me as a cautionary lesson for not taking painkillers for a caesarean section, even through the haze and confusion I was experiencing now. I continued to express milk via a pump and still had a central line in near my clavicle.

Fran had dropped in to see Callum, as well as checking in on Luca, who was being minded by Fran's mother Bernie. It was late afternoon and the rest of the ward was quiet, the various patients resting with their partition curtains closed. Across from me was an older woman, perhaps in her sixties, who was quietly sobbing. We may have different stories, but we can have similar emotional experiences. Hearing emotional pain connects us and I remember just wanting to comfort her. I made my way across to her bed and sat with this lovely, gentle lady, who was just perhaps a little confused like me. I spent the next while reassuring her that all would be okay. Looking back, although I had gone through a traumatic time myself, all I wanted was to be able to help this other person.

This was a time when Fran could finally relax, as I was out of danger. He had sat through three days of my mumblings and constant questioning, so as I was more mobile and in a general ward, he decided to take an early night away from the hospital scene and spend the evening with his brothers. As I was settling down for the night, the cannula stitched securely in place in my chest was causing me some discomfort. Sitting in my curtained cubicle, I was agitated by it. *Well, if you have an itch, scratch it,* I thought. So, I picked and picked at it. After some time, I managed to undo the stitching. Jubilant with my achievement, I sent a text to Fran, proudly announcing that I had successfully removed it. He was not happy and immediately contacted the ward to report my progress! It's hard to explain — and truly a bizarre feeling — thinking I was alright, yet not knowing what had happened or realising anything was wrong.

Discharged

On the fifth day, I was discharged from St. James's Hospital and returned to the care of The Coombe Maternity Hospital. It was lovely to hold my newborn son at last. Fran had described the events enough for me to realise that I had been through an extraordinary event and was indeed lucky to be alive to tell the tale. I was no longer confused and, though my memory still left a lot to be desired, I was now able to retain much of what I was being told.

Hugh O'Connor, who had carried out the caesarean just five days before, returned from his holiday. It's amusing to think that he'd left on the same day as I was transferred to St. James Hospital and we were both returning to The

Coombe at the same time. I joked that we'd both been on our holidays! He was ashen as he took my vitals and checked my surgery wounds. He was amazed with my quick recovery and scheduled a follow-up consultation for six weeks' time.

There was something on my mind that I needed clarifying. I'd always had the vision of having three children and it was still my plan. Would this amniotic fluid embolism impact my plans? Fran stated categorically that we were not having a third child, yet my inner voice wanted to be heard. I was matter of fact and asked Hugh, "What's the chances of this happening again, if I got pregnant?" With such conviction that it took me by surprise, Hugh replied, "You are not to have any more children. Never again, Karen." For a man with such a calm and gentle demeanour, he seemed quite stern in his response to me.

The following day, he returned a little more approachable around the whole issue of another pregnancy. In fact, he apologised for telling me to have no more children. I knew his initial sternness had been purely out of concern for me, as his patient. He'd been on the phone to St. James's Hospital every day during his holiday checking up on me. Knowing this, I tried again. "What are the statistics on women who have gone on to have another child after having an amniotic fluid embolism?" I asked. He spoke quietly and deliberately, as he glanced between me and Fran. "There are no statistics available in Ireland. It's a rare complication with no known women surviving it. We would have to look at America, and even then, it would be low. Most doctors would advise against it," Hugh said. "So it's not impossible!" I said with a smile. "No, not impossible," he agreed, reluctantly. He also agreed that the likelihood of it happening again was even more remote, since it was such a rare occurrence in the first place. That was enough for me; just knowing it was possible. For now, I would leave this subject alone and get on with my recovery.

My family and friends breathed a sigh of relief and assumed all was well when after a few days, I returned home with my baby son. We lived in a beautiful part of Co. Wicklow, just outside Tinahely, a quiet rural setting. It was over an hour's drive from our families. As a mother of two young boys and recovering from such a life-changing event, I began to feel quite overwhelmed.

Chapter 2

My Roadmap Written by a Younger Me!

"The most common way people give up their power is by thinking they don't have any."

Alice Walker

Fran and I had a long road to my recovery with many challenges to overcome, as well as having to look after our young family that included our newborn baby. Although my memory of events was beginning to return, it was events from long ago that I could begin to piece together, and the previous few weeks, in particular the few days around Callum's birth, were still hazy. I was also exhausted all the time. Tiredness like I'd never felt before. Not just newborn baby tiredness, but constant low energy, which took quite some time to lift.

There was something playing on my mind too. I wondered why I was still here. Was there a reason why I managed to survive this ordeal? Did it have a purpose? To my surprise, I felt so very angry. Angry that I was still here without knowing why or what it all meant.

As a young girl, like many young girls, I had wished for the man of my dreams. When I found this man, we'd marry, have children and start a family of our own, I thought. So, when I married Fran and started a family, I figuratively 'exhaled'. I wouldn't have to wear the mask of being an extrovert.

I could hide behind my 'mother' mask. I would like to say that motherhood solved all my problems. However, it only magnified the 'masking' of my own self. By hiding behind the motherhood mask, I was being invisible. I now know this was a theme I had been running since childhood. Trying to stay invisible to keep out of trouble and to be accepted by the adults around me. This was not the true me. The true me wanted to have a voice, to have an identity. Motherhood only added to my inner frustrations.

The journey back to visibility was going to be a challenge; I fought it every step of the way. My ingrained programming wanted me to stay small, in my own little world. I found it hard to break away from my old way of coping, yet whenever I sided with that old way of behaving, a little voice inside questioned me, *Are you being seen? Are you being heard?*

During this time, my thoughts would frequently return to my childhood. *What went wrong? How did I go from a carefree young spirit to being one that had fears and doubts?* As a child, I remember being asked, "What do you want to be when you grow up?" I probably had a different answer each time I was asked. My answer kept changing. Sometimes I would want to be an explorer; the next minute, a teacher; and at one stage, I told my uncle I wanted to be a mammy. I remember he laughed and later recounted the story to other grown-ups, saying that sure would be easy to achieve! Easy to achieve, maybe, but one of the hardest jobs, as I later found out.

As children, we believe anything is possible. We place no limits on what we can achieve. Yet ask someone who is 30 years old what they want to be and their answers may be more modest than that of their child self. What happens along the way?

In his book *What to Say When You Talk to Your Self*, **Dr. Shad Helmstetter** says that children have heard the word 'no' or been told what they 'can't do' 148,000 times before the age of 18. That amounts to a lot of negative programming. In fact, as children, we are bombarded with programming, rules, how to behave… the negative impact list goes on. It's a tough time for children. These rules and programming come from our family. Rules that set out how our own individual families want us to 'behave'. Then there are cultural norms in our society. Our schools have rules. Our government has rules. Over time, we are 'domesticated'. That lovely unique spirit of a child is 'tamed'. That beautiful being that felt everything was possible soon learned that it was *not okay to be themselves*. They had to conform in order to be accepted. And slowly, their spirit gets quashed. My spirit was quashed to a point that I felt it wasn't safe being me.

Now as a mother, I have found that I, too, have been guilty of this with my own children. As a mum to three amazing children, I found it tough. When we would go visit relatives, I would warn the children beforehand to behave. 'Behaving' amounted to being quiet and not embarrassing us! As the adult, I wanted to relax in the company of other grown-ups and not be 'on duty', minding the kids and playing referee. I can see it from the grown-up perspective, though I also recall disliking it as a child.

Growing up in my family home, my mam would have relations call in. After the initial 'hellos', I would be expected to either sit silently or leave the room. I understand that as a busy mum to four children, my own mother would have wanted some quality time with her friends and conversations that would not be appropriate for children's ears I get that now. However, as a child, it made me feel unimportant. In fact, I learned that if I wanted to stay in the room with the grown-ups, I needed to be quiet. And so, I did. As a way of being accepted by adults, I was to remain undetectable. This is one of the many belief systems that I took on as a child. It cast a shadow over my own spirit. This new way of thinking was further confirmed as being correct, when I would receive confirmation from the grown-ups. "Oh, Karen is so good. She is like a mouse. You wouldn't hear her in the house." We all like being accepted. Who likes being judged? I was learning what behaviour was *acceptable* and being quiet was one of them.

There were a few people I could 'be me' around. Some of my friends and my brother and sisters. However, they tended to get the brunt of my pent up energy! I have few childhood memories. I was the youngest of four children and idolised my big brother Liam and my two older sisters Nikki and Sharon. They just seemed so perfect to me. They always did what was right, were so wise and kind. I loved being with them. Though as the youngest, they didn't always want me tagging along! My parents were quite amazing. My father started a penfriend business and worked day and night at it. My mam worked during the day as a school secretary and was also a singer in the evenings. Life was busy in our home.

My father's childhood had a huge impact on his adult life, and as a result, my childhood. He was a child during World War II, and grew into a man inspired to find a way to promote peace and understanding across countries. My father had aspirations of becoming a journalist, though his father had other plans and this career path was not part of them. He was forbidden from attending college to pursue journalism.

On 7 April 1967, he started, what is now known as International Penfriends. His vision was to give people in all age groups, from every country, the opportunity to gain friends and increase their understanding of different cultures and communities. He also got to nurture his passion for writing. From humble beginnings in a shoe box, International Penfriends has grown to be regarded as the World's Greatest Penfriend Club, providing a medium for more than two million people aged 8 to 80+ to correspond with one another.

Unfortunately, my father had many dark shadows that he carried around with him. Sexual abuse by the clergy, as we know now, was commonplace back in the 1940s and later. My father was a victim of this, though it was not something that could be spoken, let alone help sought. This was one of the many chapters of his early life that crushed my father's spirit.

The irony is not lost on me, though it saddens me that he worked so hard to foster communication between strangers in different parts of the world, yet couldn't communicate with his own family. My father would deal with the stresses of the day through heavy drinking. His quiet demeanour would be replaced with a menacing anger. To this day, I dislike the smell of brandy and ginger ale, his drink of choice.

As a young girl, if I spoke to my father in a way that was deemed 'answering back', he would respond at a later point in time, by beating me. It would be in the evening, once my father had had his drink and his anger would rise. He would want revenge, though only when the rest of the family were out of the house. As the youngest, I would be back home early in the evenings, alone with my father, my mam still out working and the rest of the family out too. I vividly recall one fierce beating. I must have been about eight years old. I came into the house having been at a friend's birthday party. My hair was up in a ponytail which my mam had tied up with a big bow. Maybe I'd said something 'unacceptable' to my father earlier that day. When I arrived home, I didn't have my normal stealth routine activated. I came bounding in, full of laughter and excitement from a fun day and lots of sugar. Before I had time to realise that my father had been drinking, waiting, waiting for me, before I had time to react, he grabbed me by my ponytail and with the strength of ten men, swung me by my hair until I ran face first into the wall. The shock and pain hadn't registered before he repeated this against the other wall. I don't recall what he shouted at me from his drink-fuelled rage, but I knew my head was so very sore as I stumbled up the stairs to bed and cried myself to sleep. I remember brushing my hair the next morning, handfuls of hair on the brush as I delicately drew it through. He had literally pulled my hair out at the roots. My young mind tried to make sense of it. And the only logical conclusion I could come up with was that I angered my father, so there must be something wrong with me. I must be a bad person.

Whenever I was in the house alone with my father, especially if he had been drinking, I would hide in my bedroom wardrobe. Safely behind the clothes, I could hear him calling me, even come looking for me, though he never knew I was there. I can still recall the sheer panic of hearing him shout my name throughout the house. I'd hear him stomping up the stairs and approach the wardrobe. I could smell the brandy and cigarettes on his breath. Eventually, he would stop the search and fall into a drunken sleep. This, for me, was normality.

The first time we experience an emotional upset, it's just an experience. However, this experience is stored in our filing cabinet of life — our minds. As children, we also take these events personally. We ask, "What did I do to deserve this? What's wrong with me?" We make a mental note, record it in our subconscious. Our minds are like computers. They are logical in nature. They like to make rational sense of what we experience. When we experience something for the first time, an idea is formed in our mind, in this instance, perhaps, 'it's not safe being me' or 'my needs don't matter'. The mind will then be on the lookout for other events that validate this thought. And when that initial thought is validated, it moves from 'experience' to 'belief'.

You might well ask, 'Why don't our minds look for validation to show that the opposite is true?' The answer is that the opposite is not a life-threatening situation. If my existence is validated, if there are examples of where my needs *are* met, it does not benefit my safety! Our minds filter experiences through fear, doubt and judgment, always on the lookout for experiences that may *threaten* our safety.

So if a similar event occurs, and the thought is validated and strengthened, the thought 'it's not safe being me' is now not only a thought, but a belief. Our minds then recognise that these situations are to be avoided. This is an evolutionary tactic that was necessary for our survival. We needed to learn from negative experiences so we could avoid them in the future. Now in the 21st century, our environment has changed much quicker than our genetic evolution. Although we are no longer in physically dangerous situations, our brains are still scanning possible situations that threaten our survival. I have worked with many clients over the years and found this to be the case: although we have different stories, we have similar emotional experiences. Fears, sadness, anxiety, to name but a few. As such, we adopt a variety of coping mechanisms.

In 1999, I qualified as a Five Element Acupuncturist. I trained under the world renowned J.R. Worsley. One of the core tenants of Five Element Acupuncture is that the heart is the supreme controller. Love is the answer to everything. However, when we experience emotional pain, upset and hurt, and don't get to resolve this upset, we must find a way of making sense of it all. We are consistently evaluating situations and working out ways of surviving such upsets.

As children, we are bombarded with external information that we store in our memories. These memories are our building blocks of learning how to 'behave'. Our brains are busy organising information so that when we experience similar situations, we will choose the path that keeps us safe. When we experience unpleasant emotions and can't make sense of them, our mind steps in. It doesn't want us to feel hurt, so it rationalises the situation. It uses *rational lies* in order to help us survive.

We adopt many of these rational lies. And as we've explored, in my case, one of those was that it's safer to be invisible. This is a belief system that made sense to me and kept me safe. It was also verified by the grown-ups. When I was quiet, they accepted me. Throughout my early years, I tried to make some sort of sense of my surroundings. In my family circle, I learned the new rules of survival. If we behave in this way, we get attention. If we behave in this way, we get accepted.

And so, we withdraw our expectations. We withdraw our emotional needs. We cast a shadow over our brilliance, our uniqueness. We dull our spirit, 'dumb it down' in order to survive. This becomes our blueprint. Our formative years chart a 'survival map' of how to survive in this world. This map was developed by an eight-year-old or perhaps even a five-year-old, developed from a child's perspective, developed so this child can survive childhood.

What beliefs did you put in place before the age of 10? What roadmap did you create to survive childhood challenges?

Here are a few of my earlier beliefs:

It's not safe to be me.

I don't deserve love.

My needs don't matter.

It's safer to be invisible.

Again, you were probably younger than 10 years old when you formulated your view of the world and how to navigate it. These beliefs became your survival roadmap. When you had similar experiences as you get older, your mind would go to the 'filing cabinet' of experiences, pull out your 'safe' response, and you, as a result, act accordingly. These coping mechanisms will remain in place until you **go deep**, take an in-depth look at them and hit reset. These negative beliefs are like invisible chains that keep you small. They keep you from pursuing your dreams because of your past experiences.

This came to mind when I brought the children to a circus recently. I could see the amazing acrobats doing daring fantastic feats. It occurred to me that they must have believed these stunts were achievable and worked towards that goal. I saw the clowns carry out choreographed moves to entertain the audience. Again, they must have believed they could achieve this and worked tirelessly towards their goals. Just like the children, I was in awe of their strength, their courage and their ability to entertain.

During the interval, we were invited to take a look at the animal enclosures. In one area, some elephants were tethered with only a small chain. It was obvious that these magnificent animals had the strength to break free, but for some reason, they didn't. I saw a trainer nearby and asked him, "How does this small chain work?" "Well," he replied, "when they are very young and much smaller, we use that sized chain to tether them. At that age, it's enough to hold them. As they grow larger, they are conditioned to believe they cannot break away. They think the chain can still hold them, so they never try to break free." I felt a deep sadness for these majestic animals. These elephants have such potential yet here they were simply there for our entertainment, held back by a belief they took on board as a baby.

Like the elephants, I haven't attempted things on many occasions, because there was this voice in my head telling me that it wasn't safe to try something new, or that perhaps I couldn't do it. How many of us avoid trying something, because we believe we can't do it?

There have been many times in my life when people have had a negative impact on me. They might have said something that created doubt in my mind. They may not even have realised the effect and hadn't meant any malice with their words. They could have been well-intentioned friends or family who were just nervous of me trying something new. However, their words or actions somehow eroded my self-confidence and ultimately my potential.

And then there are times when people have a positive impact on us, those who support us, lift us up, like a *parachute*, sometimes without us even realising it at the time.

Let me introduce you to Lawrence Anthony. He was known as the Elephant Whisperer due to his unique ability to calm traumatised elephants. Rogue elephants, destined to be shot, were rescued and rehabilitated. Anthony passed away on 7 March 2012, having helped these beautiful animals for many years prior to his passing. When he died, 31 wild elephants began a quest. They walked for days and made their way in a solemn procession to Anthony's home. Their wonderful memory of this 'family member' evoked such an emotional act that they wanted to pay their respects and say goodbye to their beloved man-friend. When they reached his rural compound on the vast Thula Thula game reserve in South Africa, they remained in quiet reverence, then after two days, left as silently as they had arrived.

How did these animals know that he had died? Some suggest that the elephants had such a strong connection to this man that they could sense the precise timing of his passing. Those who witnessed the event could 'feel' the invisible chains of love connecting Anthony to these wonderful animals. This remained in the elephants' memory after all those years.

These two contrasting events have stayed with me.

The power of memory:

- can release our potential, when nurtured with love; or
- can hold us prisoner, when we focus on past failures.

What about our own invisible chains of failure? How do they impact us? If we nurture potential, just like Lawrence Anthony, watch what can be achieved! When we take action, the fear of failure diminishes in size and strength.

This brings to my mind my favourite Disney song "Let It Go", which has recently touched not only children, but adults too. One part of the song says:

"It's funny how some distance

Makes everything seem small

And the fears that once controlled me

Can't get to me at all

It's time to see what I can do

To test the limits and break through

If invisible chains are holding you back, *let it go, let it go."*

During sessions, I work together with clients to uncover their core negative beliefs. Once we become aware of these limiting beliefs, we remove them and replace them with a more supportive belief system. Throughout this book, you will encounter questions designed to uncover the events that established your own core negative beliefs, as well as uncovering the situations that validated those beliefs and the coping mechanisms you put in place in response to them.

Fieldwork:

Are there certain people who rub you up the wrong way or situations that make you feel uncomfortable? What are your thoughts around the person or situation? Is the thought isolated, or have you thought it before? Could this thought be a belief? That is, has it occurred before? Might this belief be part of your current belief system? If it has been in place for a long time, it may well be from your primitive childhood roadmap. Ask yourself whether this belief is serving your greater good now. It could be time to upgrade that roadmap!

What core negative beliefs do you have?

How have these been validated?

What life experiences or comments have 'confirmed' these to you?

Chapter 3

Challenges with My Inner Beliefs of Myself

"I've come to believe that each of us has a personal calling that's as unique as a fingerprint – and that the best way to succeed is to discover what you love and then find a way to offer it to others in the form of service, working hard, and also allowing the energy of the universe to lead you."

Oprah Winfrey

How often do we endorse what we say to ourselves? How did our 'inner chatter' shape us as children and young adults? What restrictions do we place upon ourselves in order to adhere to those beliefs? Once we set up a core negative belief, our minds look for proof that it's appropriate to have that belief in place.

A particular example comes to mind from when I was at school. I was about eight years old and my teacher at that time was a medium-built woman with short blonde hair. She had an abrasive tone to her voice and would screech at us from across the room. I was seated next to the window that overlooked the school yard. In the distance, I could see the Dublin mountains. Often, I would just sit there and gaze out at them, drifting off and dreaming about the many adventures I could have in those mountains or what I would do when I was all grown up. "Karen, stop daydreaming", the voice of my teacher cut through the tranquillity of my imaginings.

If you had been there, you would have seen her haul me up to the front of the class. I stood there, looking down towards my classmates, waiting for her to speak. "Tell the class what you were daydreaming about, Karen", she demanded. I stood at the top of the classroom and regaled my classmates with my explorer tales — of expeditions I'd imagined myself undertaking and of travels to far off lands — my fellow classmates enjoyed my stories. I had believed it was okay to share my fantasising with them. I loved sharing the energy. It felt freeing and expansive! "Sit down, Ms. O'Donnell, and stop daydreaming", the teacher scoffed. She gave me 'lines' to write that day. *I must not day-dream in class*, 100 times.

Unfortunately, it happened again, though this time I was hauled up to the front of the room by a now angry teacher. I felt dizzy, suffocated, as if the room was closing in on me. I said nothing. The teacher laughed at me and some of my classmates were sniggering. I just wanted the ground to open up and swallow me.

Has anyone ever laughed at your dreams?

Has anyone ever made you feel small?

Has anyone ever hurt you with just their words?

How did that feel to you?

These early experiences in school cemented two new beliefs for me. Limiting beliefs!

- It's not okay to dream;
- And speaking in front of people was painful and to be avoided at all costs.

This incident further validated my belief that by *being invisible and keeping quiet*, I would be safe. Having this in place, I became withdrawn, shy and rarely spoke in a group, even with my friends. I was eight years old when this happened, yet well into my adult life, I was still running this limiting belief. As an adult, I shied away from speaking in public. Ever.

When something doesn't go right for you, have you ever said, "I knew good things wouldn't happen to me"? Or when something has gone right, have you ever suggested, "Something bad is bound to happen", or "Don't get too excited; it won't last"? That roadmap is so strong. Even though it is trying to keep us safe, it may be counterproductive.

Your thought patterns, behaviours and actions are related to the beliefs you hold. This belief system can support you in a positive way or hold you back. The information that you feed into your brain is your mind's 'understanding'. If you have been feeding it a diet of "I'm not good enough", this will be your shadow 'truth'. This is the roadmap according to which your life will be driven.

Whatever decisions or choices you may encounter, they are all passed through this filter, this belief system, this roadmap. As such, you must question it. Is this the best roadmap for me? Is this roadmap serving my greater good? Will this roadmap lead me to my goals or to deadends? If you put your car on autopilot, you leave these decisions to be navigated along a road that was developed by a child.

Now is the time for an upgrade!

Emanuel Ninger, originally from Germany, lived in New Jersey and worked as a sign painter. He also had another somewhat nefarious occupation. He was a counterfeiter. He began his counterfeiting enterprise in the late 1870s and became known to the Secret Service as 'Jim the Penman'. He would purchase bond paper and soak it in dilute coffee to get the paper just the right colour of used banknotes. He would then align the paper over a genuine banknote and, relying on his naked eye, painstakingly duplicate the intricate detail of the note.

In 1896, his reign as king counterfeiter came to an end. He entered a bar and bought a drink with a fake note. Picking up the bill from the wet counter, the bartender noticed some of the ink on his fingers and called the police. When searching his home, they found the room where Ninger was counterfeiting money, in which there were also three portraits he had painted. These paintings were later sold for over $5000 each. The irony is that Ninger spent as much time counterfeiting a banknote as it took to paint a portrait that would sell for over $5000.

Ninger was a thief, but the person he stole from most was himself. Somewhere on his roadmap he may have picked up a belief that resulted in him doubting his own talents. How many people have their potential dreams stolen by their own primitive roadmap?

In her poem *Robbed*, Kitty Chappell writes that the "deadliest voice is not the one with the gun, but the one who tells you it can't be done". The poem is about how that little voice in our heads can rob us of our potential.

I know that I have, on several occasions, turned down opportunities that I would have liked to take. I would subconsciously consult my inner roadmap and the default answer would be 'don't do it'. In reality, I was more than capable, but fear, doubt and judgment would lead to my inner critic saying 'no'. That roadmap has kept me small. That roadmap restricted where I went and imposed deadends. It placed roadwork signs in my way and didn't let me pass. How many roads are 'out of bounds' as a result of your inner roadmap? Who put them there? And is it time to upgrade?

You may be wondering if that is even possible. Yes, these beliefs are deeply ingrained in your subconscious. However, you do not have to go through life on unconscious autopilot. If the roadmap you are following is not serving your higher purpose, the good news is that you can change your outdated signposts and upgrade it to an *innerGPS* that you can rely on.

 **Fieldwork:**

Write down the opportunities you turned down as a result of pre-programmed fears, doubt and judgment, from that early roadmap. Then on the other hand, list which of your beliefs *support* your progression in life. This will come in handy during the exercise in the Go Deep section later in this book.

Chapter 4

Our Masks and Relationships

"All the world's a stage and all the men and women merely players."

William Shakespeare

Our lives are comprised of many different interconnected and interdependent relationships. As each new relationship begins, it tends to start off well. We are all aware of the 'honeymoon' phase of these relationships. This is the time when we all put our best foot forward, presenting our best self, or at least, the self that is most acceptable by others' standards. We all bring baggage from unresolved emotional issues from past experiences into our relationships. These unresolved issues are our wounds and shadows that we feel should not be seen by others. We enter each relationship, be it personal or business, with our primitive roadmap. We put the 'honeymoon' mask on, trying to be our 'nicest' selves, all the while hiding the emotional wounds from our past.

We are asked to 'perform' on many stages. The lines we learn come from our families, our culture, our society, our schooling, our friends, etc... The list goes on and on. With the constant bombardment of expectations and judgments, we learn how to act our parts, hiding our true selves.

I learned that masks were acceptable. A mask of silence, a smile, a nod of agreement were all acceptable, even if I didn't feel that way on the inside. My mask of invisibility had many different strands to it. I might attend a group and just not contribute. If I didn't contribute, I couldn't be wrong or be judged.

I had wanted to be 'invisible' for as long as I could remember. It never really felt like I was living my life, more like that I was playing a part in various plays — going through the motions of life not really participating in it. During my teenage years, I started to question what was deemed acceptable. Why? Why shouldn't I give my opinion? I have a right to be heard. Instead of hiding away from my drunken father, I would stand up to him and answer him back. As a teenager, he was less likely to beat me, but instead would complain to my mother about me. My 'disobedience' would frequently be the reason for their arguments. As I got older, I spent less and less time at home, and started to feel I was breaking free from my father's abusive nature.

Turning 18 years old proved to be a tricky time for me, though. Traditionally the time we transition from childhood to adulthood, it can be a challenging experience. I needed to rethink my subject choices in school and decided to re-sit my leaving certificate examinations. A change in subjects required that I change school. My friends had moved on to the next phase of their lives. They were entering the workplace or attending college. I felt like I'd failed with my education, like I'd wasted so much time. I had been seeing a guy for almost five years and the relationship had recently come to an end. Even my sisters had moved on, both relocating to London. I was spending more time back at home again with my studies.

The one shining light in the dimness of my emotions was my dog Snoopy. Snoopy and I had an extraordinarily special bond. She would always bring a smile to my face, though I seemed to be crying around her more and more. Spending so much time at home meant I was around my father a lot more, which meant hearing his drunken rants frequently. Instead of hiding from him now, I was used to standing up to him. That screaming whisper within wanted to be heard. One time, I was standing in the kitchen and he took a swipe at me. I grabbed his arm and told him that if he attempted to hit me again, I would fight back. The anger in me didn't subside for some time and we continued to argue frequently. We never sat down and discussed our differences. He would just drink and get more verbally abusive. My mam was now running a successful business during the day and still singing at night. Whenever she was home, she would be greeted by my father who would complain about my attitude. That Christmas, when my sisters were home, I wanted to tell them how sad I was feeling, that I felt like such a failure. Instead, I put on my happy mask and pretended everything was perfectly fine.

After the Christmas break, they returned to London and wearing my happy mask became too exhausting, so I withdrew. I withdrew from my mam, from my friends and even from Snoopy. My anger towards my father had morphed into anger towards myself. I constantly berated myself for how my life was turning out. That negative voice kept getting louder and louder.

The anger — mine and my father's anger — was like a ticking time bomb. The tension in the house was becoming unbearable and my poor mam was caught in the middle. Any time I tried to 'rebel' against my core negative beliefs, I would fail. I didn't have the necessary emotional tools of an *innerGPS*. Each time I failed, my core negative belief was validated. Each time I failed, those voices just got stronger and stronger, telling me the solution was to become 'invisible' and that this was the safest way for me to be. The weight of carrying this constant burden came to a head that year. No-one seemed to understand me. Feeling alone, I imagined I was the cause of all the arguments at home. The thought of just 'checking out' crossed my mind several times, but I always had a reason not to - Snoopy. I didn't want to leave her. She would never understand how I could. Still, I got more depressed and had zero sense of self-worth. The reasons to remain grew increasingly faint. I could see no way out of this darkness. I planned my exit from this life.

I'd always avoided taking tablets, even for a headache, so it's surprising that this was my 'route of choice'. It seemed the easiest. Gathering a large supply of tablets from a variety of courses until I felt I had enough. Writing the note to my mam was hard, but I truly felt it would make her life easier - my dad would stop complaining about me and she wouldn't have to defend me all the time. I really thought her life would be better if I were gone. Once I made the decision, a strange calmness came over me. I'd chosen an evening that my mam was out, so I stood in the bathroom and began to take the pills. One after the other. I hated pills. But I took them. Over 100 of them. It took what seemed like an age to get to the last one and then I went to bed. When I lay down, an acceptance and relief that the pain would finally be at an end fell upon me. This was not a cry for help. This was my desire for the pain to stop. I would be a burden to my family no more.

I awoke vomiting. Violently. I vomited throughout the night and managed not to wake my mam. I'd been asleep for only a few hours before I felt so sick I could hardly move from the bathroom. A friend of my sister was staying with us. She must have heard me vomiting and came to be with me. I didn't tell her what I'd tried to do, though I think she may have had an idea. She stayed all night by my side and showed an enormous amount of empathy and concern for me. She was truly my *parachute* that night.

It's hard to explain the thoughts that pervaded my mind during those moments of utter despair. The actions that follow those thoughts aren't logical, so can't be explained logically. If my 'checking out' had worked, I would have been completely accepting of my mam finding me dead. Not in my wildest dreams would I have been okay with this. But that night I was. However, as I hadn't been successful, I did not want her finding my note or ever learning of what I had tried to do. So, I made up some story that I had picked up a tummy bug and spent the next couple of days in bed. I ripped up the note, ashamed that I had failed and not wanting anyone to know.

As well as feeling a complete failure, I was wracked with shame. I was ashamed of what I had tried to do and guilty for how my family would feel if they ever found out. In moments of quiet desperation, I still didn't have an ounce of compassion for myself. This is how destructive a roadmap can be. It wanted me to be invisible, yet I was rebelling by speaking out and standing up to my father. Then my mind had turned on me and almost made me permanently invisible.

I had become conscious of the fact that I couldn't remain living at home with my mam and dad, so I planned an exit of a different type. My two sisters were living in London and I decided to go look for work there. How often do we hear that running from problems doesn't help? However, in the short term, it helped me. In London, I could lose myself. I loved the newfound freedom and challenges that living away from home brought. This was a time of healing and also a time to find myself. I could really listen to my inner whispers and was able to get a new perspective on life. Although, I still hadn't experienced what it was like to *go deep*, the move to England had put some distance between me and my emotional baggage.

I was later to find out that emotional baggage doesn't leave you, unless you unpack it.

Chapter 5

The Opponents

"The cave you fear to enter holds the treasure you seek."

Joseph Campbell

Your core negative beliefs are in direct opposition to your screaming whisper (the voice inside telling you that you are better than this). We know that both have your best interests as their goal. Yet when these two enter the arena of your mind, they are each other's opponents, on account of going about the goal differently. They have opposite approaches to acting in your best interests and come from their own unique angle - one from fear; the other, love.

When studying Five Element Acupuncture, I was fascinated to learn of the spiritual and emotional connection between the various organs. I mentioned before that Five Element Acupuncture considers the heart as where your spirit resides. The heart is also known as the supreme controller and is where we feel our deepest love and passions. Love is the bond that connects us to each other. We know the pain of being 'heartbroken', of experiencing 'heartless' people or of 'wearing our heart on our sleeve'. We speak of feelings being 'heartfelt' or someone having a 'heart of gold'. These expressions refer to the spiritual aspect of people, which is said to reside in the heart. The heart belongs to the Fire element and is associated with warmth, laughter and enthusiasm.

Consider for a moment a snapshot of a child's life. As children, our minds are like sponges. Always taking in experiences and details. Learning how to respond or react to any given situation. Many of our experiences are loving, caring and filled with joy. We love these interactions. As children, we are quite ego-centric. The world revolves around us. We are the centre of our own world. Our focus is on ourselves. We don't have responsibilities. We just *are*! So, what happens when we have situations that are not pleasant or positive for us?

What happens when we encounter unpleasant situations, like arguing with an older sibling, but haven't developed the emotional maturity to deal with it?

Firstly, we don't know how to see the other's viewpoint. A parent may need to step in and referee, but catch a parent on a bad day when they are dealing with less trivial matters, and they may not referee as mindfully as perhaps they could. That interaction with a sibling could end up with both of you being scolded, or you alone might get blamed for the commotion, or a parent may exacerbate it and shout, "Just stop causing trouble".

Then there is no emotional resolution to the situation. Your heart is now dealing with rejection from your parent. How does a young child process this? A young seven-year-old perhaps? A young mind may see danger and not want to fall out with the person who nurtures them. This young mind might be compelled to conform and not cause trouble. This is the realm of the mind. The mind creates mechanisms to keep us safe — for our very survival. We fall out with one of our nurturers; the mind needs to step in.

The heart is concerned with love, our spiritual growth and enabling us to achieve our potential. The mind is concerned with protecting us, maintaining our existence and keeping us safe. These two superpowers are working, as best they can, *for us* to experience life and to survive life.

In psychology, *Maslow's Hierarchy of Needs*, is a five-tier model of human needs. The tiers are as follows:

1. Psychological
    2. Safety
        3. Love/belonging
            4. Esteem
                5. Self-actualisation.

According to Maslow's model, we can see that we need Safety before Love/Belonging. We need Love/Belonging before Esteem, and Esteem before Self-actualisation. As we want to be safe and accepted by others, we may choose to place part of our personality in the shadow, in order to get that sense of safety. This helps to explain why we are guided sometimes by our core negative beliefs that try to keep us safe and accepted.

Shadow-Self

Swiss psychiatrist Carl Jung (1875-1961) called this the shadow. Our shadow-self contains those dark aspects of our character that we have denied or hidden: those aspects that are deemed unacceptable by other people and even that we ourselves deem unacceptable. We hide our shadow deep in our subconsciousness, out of sight of others and even ourselves. Up until this point in our development, our heart has been the supreme controller. We feel emotions, we laugh, we cry and those who care for us support our emotional growth. When we find our natural behaviour is unacceptable to those around us, we feel pain. Not physical pain, rather emotional pain at a deeper level. We must somehow shield ourselves from this new emotional upset. We are ashamed of that side of us being seen, because we believe it to be flawed. The mind creates a way of protecting us from this pain - our alter ego. As a child, our mind sets up this protective space, like an outside shell to safeguard us from external interactions. We believe there is something wrong with us. Because of this emotional pain, we take on shadow beliefs like, "I'm not worthy of love", "there is something wrong with me" and "I'm not lovable". This ego, or *roadmap*, has been set up by a child, remember, to survive childhood interactions.

There comes a time in our adult life when our soul's whispers gets louder and louder. When we realise that the roadmap that we have been following is outdated. When we realise our ego needs to work with and not against our heart.

I, like most (if not all) of us, abandoned part of me, part of myself, part of who I really was at a heart level and spent many years hiding behind the fragile shield of this ego. I did this for many years. I sought shelter behind this shield, in the shadows, and it kept me safe during these early years of life. The wounds of my heart stayed buried beneath this shield. There were times when my soul, or *real self*, attempted to be heard, wanted me to acknowledge my own truth, begged me to open my own talents, yet I ignored it. My ego was fearful of what might happen and quickly shut down what was in my heart.

Some of the behaviours I adopted as a result of my beliefs were self-destructive, especially the judgment I cast upon myself and that monkey chatter, with which I spoke inwardly. Although my father may have been the reason that these core negative beliefs were created, it was me who continued sabotaging myself. How many times do we berate ourselves, reducing ourselves to a quivering mess? *I* did that to myself. No-one else! Whenever I attempted to speak up for myself, that inner voice would put me down, judge me, say nasty things about me. Who did I think I was? Who would listen to me? It even laughed at me.

This shadow-self can turn on you. It has the ability to control your thoughts, emotions and your behaviour. This shadow-self, which was set up to protect you from pain, goes into overdrive — a self-destruct mode — as it systematically deconstructs that which is you. Anything that jeopardises its goal of keeping you safe is thrown out as dangerous.

Of the behaviours we adopt, some are more destructive than others. For example, I was an emotional eater. If I was happy, I would celebrate with an exquisite meal; if I received some bad news, I would seek comfort in something tasty. There are many times I wanted to find a healthier way of dealing with the stresses of life, yet food was my 'quick fix'. A healthier way of handling a misunderstanding with someone, would involve me speaking up. Standing up for myself and talking through my feelings. Of course, this was intuitively the right thing to do. However, for my shadow-self, this was suicide! This was me opening up to likely ridicule, rejection or humiliation. This was me being vulnerable. My shadow-self wanted to protect me from this. It would begin with a quiet word in my ear, "Don't put yourself through that, it's not worth it." If I felt strong, my true self would retort with, "I deserve to be heard", but my shadow-self would come back stronger with, "Who do you think you are? You don't deserve to be heard". I would be reduced to confusion and anguish. It was easier to turn to the sticky bun and get some comfort from that. Emotional disconnection from the other person would create the initial upset and I would want to speak to them to reconnect. However, the shadow side would be so ruthless and threatening that I wanted to at least adhere to it to an extent, and so I would back off.

It's so easy for us to judge someone who is running a negative behaviour. It's easy to say, "Why don't they do something about it?" We all take on different behaviours as a way of coping. Some are just more acceptable than others. As Robert Louis Stevenson notes in his book *Strange Case of Dr. Jekyll and Mr. Hyde*, "Man is not one, but truly two; he has a conscious personality and a shadow, each of which often battle for supremacy within his mind." Both, however, feel they are doing what's best for the person.

As a child growing up, I did receive support and encouragement to do my best. Though, as is the Irish culture, you were not encouraged to 'speak' of your achievements. This would have been regarded as boasting and was frowned upon. Modesty was encouraged. Excel by all means but be modest! It was the expected thing to do. Although we would have been encouraged to do our best, I felt I had to hide my talents. Excelling in life was not 'acceptable'. You may find this notion completely crazy. Remember, we have a survival instinct. Our survival instinct has a 'negative' bias. It will pay more attention to situations that may threaten our existence. The withholding of love or acceptance from an adult could be that very threat and we want to avoid it. And we avoid it by people-pleasing!

Our shadow-self hides, from others and from ourselves, the qualities that we have been conditioned to believe are negative. When confronted by others displaying these qualities, we often condemn them to ensure the focus is taken away from the fact that we too possess these qualities. We relish in this false superiority, believing they are immoral and we are virtuous.

We can do this in two ways - judging others when we also are guilty of that behaviour and judging ourselves. Here are some examples:

When I see someone verbally putting down another person, I get on my high horse and I judge the abusive person. However, let's take a closer look at this in relation to myself. Have I ever put down other people? (Ehem, yes!) And have I ever put myself down? (Ouch! Now that hurts. In fact, don't I do that all the time?)

Sometimes when we feel strongly about a situation, it's because we are victims of it ourselves. And usually we are both the victim and the perpetrator.

My mam would always say, "If you point the finger at others, be aware that three fingers are pointing back to you". If you can spot a particular character flaw in others, then it's familiar to you. It's likely that this is also a shortcoming of your character. *If you spot it, you got it!* When we judge others harshly, it could be an indication of what we are doing or have done ourselves. When we react to a trait in someone else, it reflects that the trait also lives within us.

Now I check myself. If I am about to launch into finding fault with others, I *go deep* and notice what is going on there so as I can clear it or deal with it. Each time there is this feeling of judgment, I know that there is a deeper learning available to me. At the very least, I gain a sense of humility and usually a lot more.

This type of self-enquiry also works with positive traits. When you see someone being kind, the kindness that resides within you is reflected back to you. However, for those negative traits, you may need to clear this feeling. Later in the Strategies chapter, you will discover clearing techniques, including the one I use called Ho'oponopono.

Our shadow-self hides not only the behaviours that we deem ugly, but also our traits that we feel we should not reveal. The shadows hide our uniqueness, our treasures, and our positive characteristics.

Hidden Treasures

Our shadow harbours our negative behaviours and also our positive qualities — our unique selves. Throughout childhood, certain traits were frowned upon by family, schools and society. This was part of our domestication process. Positive traits such as confidence and determination could even be labelled as 'boisterous' and 'stubborn', and as such, banished to the dark side, the shadow side. Our need to be accepted by society resulted in us banishing our talents, which had the potential to make us more unique and effective.

Crabs in a Barrel Mentality is a well-known metaphor referring to a pattern of behaviour noted in crabs when they are trapped in a barrel. In short, it means, "If I can't have it, neither can you". If one crab tries to escape, its efforts will be undermined by the others, ensuring the group's collective demise. In human behaviour, members of a group will attempt to erode the self-confidence of any member who achieves success beyond the others, or halt their progress out of envy, resentment or competitive feelings.

I see this with my children. Unfortunately, our schooling model is designed to mould our youth to conform. To be uniform. To not stand out. The children come home with extra homework if they speak out of turn or show a level of exuberance unacceptable to the teacher. These types of punishment can discourage our little ones from truly being themselves. These instances can contribute to the strengthening of core negative beliefs that our children may already have in place. I would on many occasions agree with my child's approach, though I do try to have a measured perspective and look at this from the school's perspective too. I explain it this way to the children, "Follow the rules in school, but know that we support your creativity. It's okay to be different, it's okay to have a different viewpoint and it's okay to come up with a different solution."

This domestication creates uniformity in our social groups. Creativity is squashed. Uniqueness is cast out.

In 1968, George Land and Beth Jarman carried out a research study to test the levels of creativity in 1600 children. This was the same test Land had devised for NASA to help select innovative engineers and scientists. As the assessment worked so well for NASA, he decided to test children. The test was given initially to five-year olds. The children were then retested at ten years of age and again at fifteen. The results were published in his book *Breaking Point and Beyond*. The proportion of people who scored at the genius level were:-

amongst 5 year olds: 98%

amongst 10 year olds: 30%

amongst 15 year olds: 12%

Same test given to 280,000 adults (average age of 31): 2%

The shocking results of these tests revealed that we are brought up to avoid mistakes, play it safe and not risk creative ideas. We develop this mindset to conform rather than stand out.

Our shadow-self is the doorway to our own uniqueness, on which we turned our back for so many years. Our shadow is the entrance to our individuality. By clearing the shadows, we can see our true identity. In order to access this treasure trove of positive characteristics, we may need to look at some home truths:

Fieldwork:

Are we critical of others or ourselves?

Are we prone to gossiping?

Do we judge others or ourselves?

Are we envious or jealous of other people?

Perhaps we are not as nice as we think!

We may also realise that our conscious self is not always in the driving seat, that the shadow-self has been doing the steering. By being aware of our shadow side, we can clear away the shadow debris that covers our true sparkle and uncover our *innerGPS* system. When we 'own' our shadows, we acknowledge that we, too, can be jealous. We recognise times when we speak ill of others and when our words hurt people. We no longer sit in judgment and can be more compassionate towards others and ourselves. As Carl Jung said, "The shadow is the doorway to Self."

However, Carl Jung's shadow is not purely positive or negative. It is comprised of the parts of ourselves that we're disowning. By becoming conscious of who we really are, we step into real power and can master ourselves and our lives. Remember, our shadows exist to teach us, to guide us and to give us the blessing of our entire selves. They are resources for us to explore and expose. The feelings that we have suppressed are desperate to be integrated into ourselves. They are only harmful when repressed because they materialise at the least opportune times. They can seep out resulting in us over-reacting. We have all done it, reacting to something someone said or did and then afterwards realising (or it being brought to our attention) that we over-reacted.

Shadow theory states that we must make friends with our shadow selves. Our shadows are part of us, and by denying them, we give them strength.

"It is the shadow that holds the clues," says author and spiritual teacher, Lazaris. *"The shadow also holds the secret of change, change that can affect you on a cellular level, change that can affect your very DNA."*

There's an increasing amount of research to suggest that unacknowledged negative feelings that are not dealt with appropriately actually reside in different parts of our body. Various Eastern energy medicine approaches have known of this for centuries. When we look at chakras, our energy wheels, we see that the throat chakra, our fifth chakra, is all about expressing our authentic voice and speaking our truth. Acupuncturists have known about this for thousands of years. Various organs are associated with emotions:

heart — sadness/joy;

kidneys — fear/wisdom;

lungs — grief/integrity;

liver — anger/compassion;

spleen — worry/trust.

Our emotions communicate between the body/mind and our consciousness. Ignoring negative feelings such as sadness, frustration, and anger, and pretending they don't exist means that you're not dealing with your feelings. It's just removing the battery from your fire alarm without putting out the fire. You're simply stuffing them away inside, where they are likely to fester. The ancient Hawaiians spoke about a 'black bag' that we all have inside of us. Each time we feel a negative or unhappy emotion and we don't want to deal with it, we stuff them into our black bag and pull the drawstring tight.

In 2003, I met a woman named Brandon Bays, who created a process called The Journey. By actively clearing out her emotional baggage, she recovered from a very large tumour within seven weeks. Her belief is that emotional memories are stored in the cells of the body and get passed on from one cellular generation to the next. When negativity is passed on through the cells, part of the cells' vitality shuts down. These are the areas where illness is likely to occur. I was fascinated with her work and I wanted to know more about how she cured herself of cancer and a tumour the size of a basketball. I studied with her and became an accredited Journey Therapist in 2005.

Higher Self

When I use the term 'higher self', I'm referring to the all-knowing part of you. It's that intuitive part that holds wisdom and divine truths. Your higher self can access this wisdom and divine truth to uncover your innate knowledge. This is your superpower that cannot be wounded by prejudices or judgments. It guides you intuitively, teaches you through insight and excites you with inspiration.

Your higher self is non-judgmental and looks at life without your wounds or unpleasant experiences. It views the world through optimistic and trusting eyes. Many have referred to the higher self as your 'Godlike' self for these reasons. It is true positivity. This higher self is the sum of the best parts of you and is you at your purest level. Your higher self is always there for you and will always uplift and shower you with love and kindness.

Your higher self is looking for opportunities for you to 'awaken' to the truth, to *go deep* and clear out the debris.

Shadow-Self versus Higher Self

In order to reach our chosen destination, or even decide where to go, we have a road to travel, yet the navigation equipment for planning our route is defective. Our internal driving mechanisms are not working in our favour. We are using an old roadmap, but the terrain has changed a lot since we were children.

On one hand you have your higher self, which is assured and quiet, and can intuitively guide you. The shadow-self is loud and full of its own self-importance, which often needs you to seek someone else's approval and validation. It compares you to others, creating self-doubt. Your higher self can build self-esteem, whereas your shadow-self is condescending and ultimately reduces self-esteem. Your higher self is associated with positive emotions, yet shadow-self is more associated with negative emotions.

In every quarrel, every argument, every war, each side ultimately believes they are on the right side. The same can be said of your shadow-self and higher self. Your shadow-self programmed your early experiences into existence and believes it is acting in your childhood interests. The good news is *you* put it in place, so you can alter it to serve you in a more positive way.

We have all written our own story, each with a hero and a villain. In many stories, the villain goes through a transformation. In your story, you can always alter the characters and control the outcome.

By rolling up our sleeves, being willing to sift through the debris and walking out from the shadows, we can reveal our hidden treasures. Take a listen to Karen Taylor Good's song *"Perfect Work of Art"*. In this beautiful song, she sings of how the sculptor Michelangelo just had to excavate David. David was already there and Michelangelo just had to remove the debris. She goes on to sing about the perfect soul we have deep within us. Although it is covered with negative feelings, like

52

fear, doubt and judgment, the real self is crying to come out. It's a beautiful song to check out and hear how you truly are a 'perfect work of art'. You just have to undergo an 'excavation' to reveal your true self!

 **Fieldwork:**

"Spot it… Got it!"

Stage 1

Write down the name of the person who most irritates you.

What irritates you most about ____(name)____?

What has ____(name)____ done to you?

What behaviour should ____(name)____ change?

Write without filtering your answers. Write with wild abandon!

Example — your boss

What irritates me most about <u>my boss</u> is that he is such a rude person.

<u>My boss</u> takes me for granted.

<u>My boss</u> should change how he interacts with people.

Stage 2

Using your answers from Stage 1, insert *your* name in place of the person you've chosen. Give three examples that reinforce each comment.

Example

Replace "my boss takes me for granted" with "I take me for granted".

I take me for granted by:

a) not taking adequate exercise

b) not eating healthy foods

c) not getting enough sleep

Stage 3

Then decide to rectify this.

I can rectify these by:

• Walking daily for 30 minutes

- Bringing a healthy lunch to work
- Getting to bed by 11pm

Once you stop the blame game, you are taking back responsibility for your own growth. How cool is that?

Chapter 6

Becoming Visible

"You may encounter many defeats, but you must not be defeated. In fact, it may be necessary to encounter the defeats, so you can know who you are, what you can rise from, how you can still come out of it."

Maya Angelou

What is the true cost of the coping mechanisms we have created and nurtured as a response to judgment? Being a muted version of ourselves, rather than a true version. Judging ourselves, rarely arriving at a favourable opinion. This all affects our heart space, our individual spirit, which is what makes us ourselves. We learn that being ourselves is not going to be acceptable. We wear the mask of acceptability and that which makes us truly ourselves is cast into a shadow or behind the mask.

This is how, by age 10, we have put many coping mechanisms in place. Some we put in place to cope with various situations we encountered and others are thrust upon us by our elders! Before 10 years old, we have accepted this and conformed. Then at about the age of 12, we start questioning. We question this 'domestication'. We enter the rebellious years of a teenager, when we attempt to put our own stamp on our life! We are not only fighting against life, but also negotiating with a set of core negative beliefs that have become our default programming. Our very essence — that which makes us unique — is now fighting for survival, because our identity, our very existence, is at stake here.

So we rebel. Our brilliance tries to shine through all the crud we have placed on top of it to mute it. Our spirit screams to be heard and seen. We fight, we scream, sometimes silently from the depths of despair, but we scream somehow. We want to be seen as the real person we are, not the muted version we have become.

The teenage years are a trying time for all. It's a difficult time for the young person who is seeking out their individuality, for the parent who wants the child to be accepted and for society who wants us to conform. This just serves as more validation to the mind that we need to adhere to the core negative beliefs. We need to dumb down our feelings, and then we won't get hurt by this big bad world. It's not surprising that so many of our teenagers look to taking their own lives as a solution, feeling like they've just had enough.

Our society is littered with amazing people who just were not 'accepted' as themselves, and because of this, have numbed their feelings in a variety of ways — some more socially acceptable than others. Workaholics, shopaholics, foodaholics, cleanaholics are just a few ways that we see people dumbing down their emotions, but other numbing ways can include turning to drugs and alcohol. Most turn to these vices to numb the feelings of rejection, and then society casts them further away. And so the cycle of negative validation continues.

My own journey back to visibility was a challenge, as I fought it every step of the way. I'd been happy to help others become more visible, though not myself. I had been involved in the healing therapies since 1999. I was not a stranger to the negative baggage that we can accumulate from childhood and had been seeing clients as a positive mindset coach for a couple of years, helping them clear out obstacles in their lives. More and more, *I felt a fraud.*

Let me give you some of the background:

From a young age, I was always drawn to animals. I guess they don't judge you. I always had dogs. I worked as a veterinary assistant during my teenage years and returned to this job with the same veterinarian in my twenties. Tom Farrington is an amazing person and an incredible veterinary surgeon with such a love of animals. I spent several years working with Tom. Then in my late twenties, I decided it was time to switch focus. I got a job in HR, which was only meant to be temporary. I worked at that company for almost 16 years. Before joining, I hadn't ever seen myself in an office and wanted to work with people on a more personal level. When I decided to *go deep* with my feelings around this, I realised that this meant working with people on a spiritual level. In some way, I wanted to help people heal, though not just physically.

Tom, as well as being one of the most respected veterinarians in the country, was also a homeopath. I found his approach highly engaging and so began my interest in complementary therapies. Tom would work with these enormous books, listing reams and reams of symptoms with their associated remedies. I preferred a hands-on approach and I was drawn to Five Element Acupuncture. This was a therapeutic system that involved supporting people physically, energetically and spiritually. At the time, training in Five Element Acupuncture was not possible in Ireland, but I found a three-year part-time course in the UK and travelled at weekends to Leamington Spa. I loved the course. I was privileged to be studying with an amazing group of people. I developed close friendships during that period. We all started helping people, initially through the college clinic and then later within our own private practices. I loved being able to gauge someone's energy level, making adjustments by needling various points and feeling a difference in the pulse. I found it magical and humbling to be able to support patients in such a way.

However, one thing I found frustrating was that you could support a patient by adjusting their energies, get them back to a good place, then by the next session see that their energy was back to where it had been when they started. From my childhood, listening was a skill that I had developed inadvertently. I became adept at listening to people. In the clinic room, I'd listen to what my patients were saying and what they were 'not' saying. I realised that my patients not only needed support through acupuncture, but also skills for dealing with the world they occupied. Whether it was getting aggravated at work or arguing with loved ones, I felt I needed to do more to help them.

This started my journey down a variety of studies beginning with counselling skills through Maynooth College in Co. Kildare, but I wanted something more spiritual. In 2003, I was introduced to the book *The Journey* by Brandon Bays. This book was so impactful for me. It blew my mind. It explained our emotional wounds and the journey back to ourselves. I decided to attend a weekend workshop on this amazing process. This wonderful 'guided introspection' resonated greatly with me. Although initially I attended this workshop for my own personal reasons, it quickly became clear how advantageous this process could be to my patients, so I committed to training with Brandon Bays and become an accredited Journey Therapist. The qualification involved much soul-searching and undergoing months and months of intense process work.

I remember one of the first 'processes' I had working with a facilitator. The idea is that you have a guided introspective journey. With eyes closed, you are led into a deeply meditative state where you can access deeper parts of your consciousness, clear out old emotional wounds and reframe past experiences. Ideally, you would connect with your feelings and the process would take approximately two hours. However, I just stayed in my head, not allowing myself to surrender to the process. After two hours, my patient facilitator asked me, "Karen, what's the worst that can happen if you just go with it?" To this I replied, "My mind would lose control". He then asked, "Karen, what's the best that could happen if you just went with it?" To my astonishment I said, "My mind might lose control!"

With this revelation, I surrendered to the process. It was difficult facing those childhood wounds. They were so ingrained and had led me to confront my core negative beliefs head on. It was painful confronting my father in the situations that came up while I was undergoing this process work. As I remembered those earlier experiences of confrontations, beatings and hiding from him, I realised it would be a challenge to forgive him. I fought the forgiveness as I didn't want to 'let him off the hook', but by not forgiving him, I was not allowing myself to move on. My journey was slow and I resisted until my mind finally saw that forgiving him was all for my greater good.

Throughout The Journey accreditation period, I immersed myself in some profound work and felt lighter for having done it. When you get real with yourself, you can develop such strong relationships. I connected with the kindest people on those courses. Two phenomenal women are still great friends today. Mary Hayes and Adrienne Barlow supported me, encouraged me, laughed with me and cried with me every step of the way. These amazing women have been my *parachutes*, providing me with emotional support as I've delved further into the real me.

I'd had a taste of awareness of my primitive roadmap. I had even visited the various emotional hangouts on that primitive roadmap and started getting in touch with the real me. I didn't, however, completely let go of these events. I didn't want to forgive certain people. I didn't feel they deserved my forgiveness. And as I finished up the training and focused more on helping other people overcome their obstacles, life started to get in the way again and I stopped working through my own stuff so much.

My near-death experience was a year after I qualified as a Journey Therapy practitioner. When I had the realisation that I was still running my invisibility belief, I really had to do some soul-searching.

What was I doing? I was completely present when facilitating clients through their work, but I was not really carrying out the work on myself. I seemed to be just going through the motions when it came to me. *I felt a fraud.*

I liken it to peeling an onion. I would remove a layer and then leave the onion, thinking I had done the work. Yet some months later, I would see the old pattern or recognise some old hurts and realise I had more layers to remove.

My dear friend Mary recommended a book called *Radical Forgiveness* by Colin Tipping. The title did not appeal to me at all. I bought the book and put it up on the bookshelf. The book sat on the shelf for a few months. My stubbornness had me thinking that I could complete this work without forgiveness. I'd regularly look at the book as I passed the bookshelf. It sat there on the shelf taunting me, almost saying, "So, you think you can move on without letting go?" One day, I picked up the book and found that I couldn't put it down. It resonated with me completely. From reading that book, I knew I needed to forgive my dad.

Again, as always seems to be the way, I decided that I wanted to know more about Radical Forgiveness. I had the opportunity to train with Colin Tipping and grasped it with both hands. In 2007, I qualified as a Radical Forgiveness Coach. This work complemented and enhanced the therapies I already practised and also enabled me to re-evaluate the possibilities of forgiveness. Colin Tipping, a remarkable teacher gained his angel wings on June 28th 2019. I am forever grateful for the phenomenon 'Radical Forgiveness' which was truly instrumental along my own healing journey and that of so many others. Fly high Colin.

A couple of days before my son Callum's first birthday, I got a terrible phone call from the hospital where my father was a patient. He was staying at the same hospital that I had attended the previous year after the amniotic fluid embolism. My father had been unwell and had taken a sudden turn for the worse. And now, here I was visiting him, in the same hospital, almost a year to the day after I'd been so ill. This time my father was right in front of me. Until now, I'd simply used various strategies to process my feelings around my father, but now here was this frail man with his family all gathered around his hospital bed. He had spent the past few months in the hospital and a recent test revealed lung cancer. My father had always dreaded cancer. Although we asked that he not be told, their policy was to inform patients. From the diagnosis on, he literally gave up. He stopped eating, stopped hoping. We were told he had a matter of days at most. At the end of this evening, when he was settling down for the night, I suggested I stay with him. I curled up on a chair at the end of his bed, and although it was not possible to exchange words with him, I said, "Dad, I forgive you. I am so sad and sorry for you that you had to carry your wounds and hurts around until now". All I felt in that room was love for him and regret that he never had the opportunity to be released from his childhood shackles, those shadows that cast dark clouds over his life, right to the very end. I felt complete empathy for him and wanted him to know that I forgave him and that I would have wanted a better life for him.

My father passed away at 6am on 3 August 2007

Almost a year to the day after I'd had my incredible wake-up call. I felt that year was spent well. I got to work through a lifetime of upset, I got to clear out the feelings I had for my dad and I got to reach a place of understanding and love.

When I used to think of my dad, a huge wave of anger would wash over me. Having done Journey work and Radical Forgiveness, that anger is now gone and has been replaced with empathy, compassion and love.

Why am I telling you all this? When I had my near-death experience, it served as a harsh reality check. I believed I had worked through my emotional baggage, yet I realised that I had only just scratched the surface. When I was strong enough, I resolved to continue uncovering challenges in my old roadmap. In the process of doing so, I developed a system, the *innerGPS* system to guide you in making decisions that are true for you. A system that connects you to your truth, and from this truth, gives you the tools and strategies to build an authentic relationship with yourself and others.

PART II

Navigation Equipment GPS

GO DEEP

Chapter 7

Core of the Matter

"Your beliefs become your thoughts, your thoughts become your words, your words become your actions, your actions become your habits, your habits become your values, your values become your destiny."

Gandhi

Throughout our lives, we receive what I call those *screaming whispers* from our spirit. Many times, we ignore them. Keeping up appearances for others takes up too much of our energy. This energy spent keeping the old roadmap in place affects every aspect of our lives. It suffocates our own spirit, it destroys our relationships with others and ourselves, and it prevents us from fulfilling our dreams.

Our *screaming whispers* usually start around our teenage years when we question the established 'rules'. Those *screaming whispers* also bubble up when we start working, when we fall in love, when we have children. These relationships and events can lead to many doubts and uncertainties about the way we view ourselves, life and others. We often will start probing our core negative beliefs.

However, for many people, an event presents itself, an event where the burden of those early wounds and emotional pain need to be released. We reach a time in our lives when the old roadmap has far too many roadblocks and we need to take a closer look. We need to upgrade our mapping, because the well-worn paths are not taking us where we want to go. We need an *innerGPS.*

By *going deep,* we can discover a wealth of talents. By putting on our Explorer hat, we can shine a light on the depths of our being and bring our hidden treasures into the light.

Core Negative Beliefs:

I have shared with you how our core beliefs are established. Let me give you a quick synopsis here before we *go deep.*

Core beliefs were indoctrinated into us by parents, teachers, culture and society. Some were positive and others were negative. Based on negative experiences, we also took on board our own conclusions about ourselves, about others and about the world in general. From these core negative beliefs, we subconsciously created our own primitive roadmap to guide us on our journey through life. This roadmap dictates our thoughts, actions and ultimately our destiny. We created it in our childhood to help us survive situations, to help us fit in as we tried to make sense of our environment. The beliefs we took on board as children may well have been valid then, but require updating as we gain maturity, as our circumstances change. These core beliefs can be negative, though they are not *bad.*

To illustrate, think of a child who has a younger sibling and is receiving less attention from a tired worn-out parent. That child may take on a negative belief that he is unlovable. This is not true, but it helps him make sense of the situation. Consequently, he may not seek attention to avoid getting emotionally hurt by this perceived rejection. This belief resulted in less emotional pain as the child isn't looking for validation or love as much. That negative belief helped him and was more beneficial than the need to feel good about himself. These old beliefs can continue to have a powerful influence over his life, yet this belief is hidden in his subconscious.

Another example is that someone who has had a traumatic experience may take on a belief that the world is not safe. As a result, she may run many limiting beliefs based on that idea, such as restricting the relationships she may have, the places she goes or the things she does.

A further situation that we could look at is one where parents got divorced and the child may try to rationalise it. *If a parent could leave me,* they think, *I must be unlovable!* Again, that is not the case at all, but to a young child, this may be how he translates this.

When we encounter emotional hurt, the mature approach would be to resolve it. The supreme controller, the heart, is all about connection and love, and wants to clear up this upset. However, as children, we don't have the emotional maturity to process this emotional pain and work through it. The mind steps in. It has a solution. It can set up a mechanism that will reduce our exposure to emotional pain and keep us safe. A two-part mechanism exists. Firstly, a core negative belief is created; and secondly, a coping mechanism.

Examples of Common Core Negative Beliefs

I am unlovable	Life is not fair
My needs don't matter	Other people are more important than me
It's not safe being me	I must obey or suffer
I'm a failure	No matter how hard I try, it's never enough
People can't be trusted	People always abandon me
The world is not a safe place	It's not good to be outgoing

Simple Ways to Spot a Negative Belief

As a specialist in cognitive behavioural therapy (CBT), I assist clients in exploring what is keeping them in painful patterns by *going deep* and uncovering limiting beliefs. These negative beliefs can then be discarded and they can discover their own true gems. For sessions where we *go deep*, I have found some excavation tools that I share here so that you can use them to uncover your own limiting beliefs and discover your hidden gems. There are a few ways to check for potential limiting beliefs.

Self-Talk

Have you ever observed how you talk to yourself? Do you put yourself down? Are you running a belief about yourself on autopilot? When you take a wrong turn (literally or metaphorically) or make a mistake, do you criticise yourself? What are the words that you use?

Compliments

How well do you accept compliments? Do you have difficulty in accepting or believing positive comments about yourself? Notice your behaviour or internal dialogue when you receive a compliment.

Overreacting

These negative beliefs are usually associated with strong emotions and so another simple way of recognising them is when you overreact emotionally to a situation. Does your emotional response appear out of proportion to the event? After the event, do you realise you overreacted, or play the blame game and point the finger of responsibility towards others?

Triggers

A common pattern of behaviour around negative beliefs is having a fight, flight or freeze response to situations. Certain events, sounds, comments, experiences, or people trigger a reaction in you. This trigger may be how someone looks, a familiar sound, even someone's emotion. Sometimes a familiar song, phrase or even scent can be a trigger. It can be instantaneous, activating your negative core belief and the childhood memories associated with it.

You may notice a shift in your energy or your reaction may be quite intense. It's usually directed outwardly towards other people. Does any of this sound familiar?

People-Pleasing

Do you find you help other people in order to 'feel better'? Are you seeking recognition or acceptance from the people you help? By others valuing you, can you only then see your own worth?

Each core belief is an energy state and is stored in your body as well as your subconscious mind. They are childhood wounds that cannot be healed by applying rational thinking. These repeat out-of-control behaviour patterns (over-reactions) can be automatically triggered by similar words or events.

When this happens and you feel someone or something has 'pushed your buttons', this is an invitation for you to explore what's hidden beneath. This is an opportunity for you to *go deep*, find the associated belief, heal the wound and uncover hidden treasures. A negative belief will remain in place and continue to exert a powerful influence over you unless you *go deep* and clear it out.

Fortunately, it is possible to identify and clear these out with the first of our navigational stages, *going deep*. But what does this look like? Imagine for a moment you decided to go on an expedition to a place you have never been before and then someone gives you an outdated roadmap. Would you take it? An old map that you couldn't even work out where *you* were located? One where you couldn't recognise any landmarks? Or would you rather use a sophisticated GPS system that knows exactly where you are located, understands your relationship to your surroundings and all you needed to do was to key in your destination? A system that responds to potential roadblocks and reroutes you accordingly? Which would you choose?

Well, you have an *innerGPS* and it's time to activate it, initially by *going deep*.

Go Deep!

As mentioned previously, beliefs are the foundation on which we create and shape our experiences, the structure on which we build our perceptions, emotions, thoughts and experiences. When you shine a light on them and question them, they lose their power. Some people travel to far off lands and across oceans to find exotic treasure. However, for some of us, the best treasures lie just under the surface.

Do you know what your limiting beliefs may be? Would you like to? Would you like dive deep beneath the waters and get a real view of the iceberg? Become an Explorer into your own beliefs and you will unearth the reasons these beliefs were put in place, the particular patterns that have been repeating throughout your life, then clear away the debris and uncover your hidden treasures.

Go deep and discover subconscious beliefs, study them, discover where they came from and how they make you feel. Once you have an awareness of them, you can then choose whether to keep these beliefs or release them. The beliefs that support your growth and help you achieve your life's purpose, these you will keep. However, you can let go those that do not support your life's purpose or ultimate happiness.

When you begin to *go deep*, your perception changes. It's like you're accustomed to trying to use the old outdated map, having to figure out where you are and stumble around the obstacles as best you can. However, you can now upgrade to a system that assists you to navigate to your destiny. You just need to let it know where you want to go. All that is required is that you uncover and delete the beliefs that you don't want and replace them with beliefs that support the life you want to achieve. Each time you clear away the debris of negative beliefs, you uncover more gems in your ocean garden.

During one-to-one sessions with clients, I have facilitated deep-diving expeditions, where they have accessed their *innerGPS* system. Here, I would like to share with you some tools that you can use in the comfort of your own home.

Dip Your Toes into Deep Waters:

The short exercises that follow will give you material to work on during your deeper exploration!

A good way of getting in touch with your limiting beliefs is to take a blank piece of paper and draw a line down the centre of the page. Now think of something you want to achieve or obtain. Is it a goal? A dream job, a fantastic holiday, a loving relationship?

On the **right side** of the page write down as many reasons as you can think of why that 'goal' is already yours and what attributes you have that can assist you in achieving your dreams (such as integrity, hard-working, qualifications, personal traits).

Disneyland Holiday	
Why I can't achieve this....	Why it is achievable....

On the **left side** of the page write down as many reasons as possible why you won't be reaching that goal any time soon. As you write on the left, avoid filtering what you are writing. Just keep writing. The longer you write, the deeper your responses will become.

The left-hand side is what's holding you back. There may be reasons you can't achieve your goal right away, some material reasons maybe, such as not enough money. However, as you continue to write, you will notice reasons that are a little deeper. Beliefs such as 'I'm not good enough' or if a phrase begins with *"I can't"* – these can highlight a potential core negative belief. This is the beginning, as each core belief can start this way.

After 30 minutes of writing, look at the page and see which items on the list are emotionally charged. These are the ones that are statements about you. For instance, 'good things don't happen to me', 'no matter how hard I try, it's never enough' or 'my needs don't matter'. These examples conjure up a feeling and it's directed at you personally. Put a circle around the one you feel has hindered your progress the most. Choose this core negative belief and let's work on that for the rest of this workbook.

Let's Go a Little Deeper!

Self-Talk

When you drive somewhere new and make a wrong turn, what do you say to yourself? Is your self-talk reassuring you with, "Ah, that's okay, we all make mistakes. You're doing your best"? Or do you think negative comments about yourself? Take a few moments to consider situations that are new to you and how your self-talk goes in those situations.

List the likely reply or common negative phrases you use.

I am so....

I can't....

I don't....

I never....

Compliments

When someone gives you a compliment, do you accept it, or do you play it down or put yourself down? How do you feel when someone gives you a compliment?

I feel....

Overreacting

How do you react when someone pushes your buttons?

71

I can react in these ways:

Family History

Choose a number between 1 and 10. Focus on that age and jot down any upsetting event that you can recall from around that time.

How did it make you feel?

As a result of this experience, what conclusion did you make about:

Yourself...

Other people...

Life in general...

The world...

People-Pleasing

As children, we try to fit in. We discover that some behaviours are more acceptable than others. By behaving in a particular way, we can receive rewards. We learn what is acceptable. Even if we know it's not in our best interest, we can go out of our way to please others.

 Write up a list of 'good deeds' you did for others so that you would be accepted by them or recognised. Also write a list of good deeds that went unnoticed.

Good deeds to gain recognition/acceptance

Feelings when they went unnoticed

Having completed the earlier exercises, you may be aware of likely core negative beliefs that you are running. Let's *go deep* into one now.

Old beliefs were put in place to help the younger you. Uncover them with curiosity and compassion. Find a quiet place, away from noise and distractions. Turn off mobiles and other devices. Take a piece of paper and write down events in your life that are painful for you to recall. Write them out without filtering. Just write with wild abandon.

When you have finished writing, check your page and circle the event that has the highest emotional charge for you.

Event is:

 Write out your understanding of this event and how it affected you:

Who upset you?

To clear out this emotional pain, imagine the person who caused you distress is sitting across from you. Allow the younger you to speak from that hurt. Speak candidly. The objective here is to validate the feelings of the younger you. Let the younger you (which could be you of yesterday or 20 years ago) express those feelings and know that they are validated and heard by present-day you.

When you have identified the negative feelings, let the other person know, during this process, how they should have treated you. As this process work can be years after the actual event occurred, it serves no purpose confronting the person in question. However, as part of your return to health, you can take on board the actions that the other person 'should have done' and give these to yourself. For instance, if you say the other person should have been more loving, then you find three ways you can be more loving towards yourself. In this way, you are providing your own emotional growth. When coming up with actions that you can do for yourself, make them simple, small steps.

For instance:

- Mentally: Use more uplifting comments.
- Physically: Have a 20 minute walk during your lunch break.
- Spiritually: Listen to uplifting music for 15 minutes each morning.

These steps need to be achievable and simple.

Survival Kit

Once you see your own negative beliefs, you can then balance them with more supportive positive beliefs. Here's how.

When you uncover a core negative belief, take a few moments to acknowledge how it helped you survive certain situations when you were younger. Recognise how clever the younger you was for putting this in place. Take a moment to appreciate the way the old belief helped you as a child. Thank it for the part it played in keeping you safe.

Give yourself permission to let this old belief go as it no longer serves your greater good.

You will find that you'll stop 'reacting' to certain words or events. You will have this new awareness of why you react in such a way. You will find yourself making powerful, positive changes to your life. Clearing out these old negative beliefs will increase your self-confidence as you install and develop your *innerGPS*. You will heal those wounds of deep emotional pain. You will discover quicker routes to your destination. You will make healthier choices for yourself along your journey. You will find more love, success and happiness. You will enjoy sharing your journey with more supportive people.

Chapter 8

Treasure Hunters

"There's no inner landscape in the invisible world of our souls and hearts but is full of the most melodious and nourishing and wild freedom. And everyone should go there, to the wild place, where there are no cages, where there are no tight rooms without windows and without doors. Everyone should go to the free clearance places in their own hearts."

John O'Donohue

So, we know that the mind has set up a two-step process: a core negative belief followed by a coping mechanism. In fact, from that first step of setting up the core negative belief, several different coping mechanisms can be attached, depending on the situation. With the mind's intervention, the two-stage process was put in place for good reason: the core negative belief for trying to logically understand why our needs were not met, then the coping mechanism to reduce further hurt, to shut down a part of ourselves. That part is uniquely us, the part we identify with, and we learn to mute it or squash it into a version of ourselves that our child mind deemed more 'acceptable'. So the slow erosion of our uniqueness takes place.

This two-step process can affect all areas of our lives. It may have been set up to protect us; however, this primitive process does not have an 'off' switch. When we get older, it just continues to exert its control over our life.

My belief that 'it's not safe being me' led me as a child to adopt mechanisms that ensured my safety. This belief was the root of several of my mechanisms, the purpose of which is to stop me 'feeling' the impact of the belief. Let me walk you through one of them here. I adopted a coping mechanism of making myself invisible. I would physically hide from my father. This mechanism was so deep-rooted, it almost became a self-fulfilling prophecy after my son Callum's birth.

Go Deep Process

Now we are going to start the *go deep* process with a 'journey' into the body to find out your likely coping mechanisms and where they reside. Of course, you can come back to this exercise over and over when you wish to *go deep* and do more work. Indeed, during one-to-one sessions, I facilitate a much deeper process of clearing out the negative feelings. I help you install your *innerGPS* and support you in reaching your goals. In this book, I am simplifying these processes into easy-to-follow exercises. Let's get started.

Ask a friend to read out this exercise to you, access the online audio version, or record it yourself and play it back, stopping the recording when you need to *go deep*. This exercise is not to be read out yourself, as you will need to have your eyes closed throughout the exercise.

Allow 30 minutes for this exploration. From your list from the previous chapter, choose what core negative belief you would like to work on. Seek answers from your body, from your feelings, not your thoughts. This exploration process is done with a sense of curiosity and compassion. Your subconscious loves imagery, so go along with it and have fun.

The 'script' contains markers [ ] for you to pause and wait for the answer. Alternately, you can download an audio file so as you can listen to this process **https://innergpssystem. com/go-deep-process/.**

Find a quiet place, away from noise and distractions. Turn off mobiles and other devices. Take a few moments to let your mind relax. Close your eyes. Put out an intention to the universe that your *go deep* process is effortless, that it clears away some debris from the belief you want to work through, and that this exploration uncovers more joy and more of your authentic 'you'.

Take a few deep breaths in and out, and allow your body to relax. Imagine putting on your *exploring light* cap.

Bring your awareness to each part of your body. Start with your feet - see them relaxing, releasing all the stresses of the day, and thank this part of your body for the amazing work it does. Move up to your knees, your thighs, your torso, eventually moving to all parts of your body.

When you have greeted all parts of your body, you can then *go deep*. Imagine entering your body through your crown chakra, your fontanelle, that spot on the top of your head. Bring your focus inward. Become aware of your breath.

From a place of openness, silently scan your body. Imagine stepping into your heart space. Take a few moments to thank it again for keeping you alive, for creating joy and happiness, for giving you compassion and empathy.

From here, send out a request for a guide or mentor to explore with you. This guide or mentor can take various forms. It can be someone you trust, whose wisdom you trust, and who you feel safe with. It can be a higher energy. Whichever appears for you is fine.

Greet your guide, then ask:

In relation to this negative belief, if it's stored somewhere in my body, where might that be? [ ]

Wait for a feeling or an answer, then bring your focus to that part of your body. Again, approach this area with respect, curiosity and compassion. Describe how the area looks to you. Invite that part of you to communicate with you in consciousness.

Firstly, thank this part of you for making itself known to you and for helping you to understand what it's doing.

Then ask that consciousness the following:

How long has this mechanism been in place? [ ] Thank you.

Who put it in place? [ ] Thank you.

With compassion and curiosity, ask:

If there were any benefits to having this belief in place, what might they be? [ ]

(As an example, benefits of me being invisible might have been: people wouldn't notice me; I would be left alone; no one would be angry with me; I would get less upset; I would experience less pain.)

Then ask:

By having this mechanism in place, what has it prevented me from doing? [ ]

What has the cost been to me, by keeping this in place? [ ]

(In my example of cost, I might imagine: I can't be seen — when I stay in the background, people can't see me; I can't be heard — when I am in the background, no one listens to me; when upset, I chose to mute my feelings – no one knows I am upset and feelings are not resolved; I don't take opportunities — I stay small and I can't follow my interests; being invisible cost me being me.)

Thank this inner part of your body for sharing this with you. The cost usually contains your hidden treasures.

Ask your guide:

Does this mechanism still serve my higher good? [ ]

This mechanism has had some negative effects on you and your life.

Ask your guide:

When would be a good time now to release it and let it go now? [ ]

Thank this part of your body for the part it played in keeping the mechanism in place. Let it know you don't need this mechanism anymore. Imagine a window opening and the old mechanism leaving your body through this window.

Seek advice from your guide. Ask it to suggest at least three alternative behaviours that can be of benefit to your growth. These need to be small practical steps that you can carry out easily. [ ]

Thank your guide.

Then ask:

Is there anything I need to do in order to carry out these supportive habits/behaviours? [ ]

Now check in with the part of your body that housed the mechanism and enquire whether taking on board one of these new behaviours would make it more content.

If the feeling is 'no', go back to your guide and ask for three more behaviours. Continue this until the body part agrees with one of the new behaviours.

Thank this place in your body.

Ask your guide for any advice it has for you on moving forward with your new behaviour. Picture yourself waking up tomorrow, free from the outdated old coping mechanism and working with the new positive behaviour. Imagine how you will feel. How does it feel to be free from that old mechanism?

Now step into your future, one week from now. You have been living free from this old mechanism and actively working with the new positive behaviour. Breathe in the wonderful benefits that you now enjoy. See yourself interacting with others. Feel your confidence soar.

Step into the future, one month from now. See yourself more confident and happier as you fully integrate this new supportive behaviour.

Step into the future, three months from now. Imagine a situation arising that would previously have led to you reacting from the old mechanism. See, hear and feel yourself responding more positively from your new perspective. Feel how the situation plays out more positively.

Step into the future, six months from now. Notice how totally free you are from that old mechanism. What other healing has taken place? In what ways has your life changed for the better?

Allow yourself to bask in the consciousness of the future you.

Now open your eyes and come back into the room, *knowing* that *all* of these treasures are within you. You just need to access them.

When you have opened your eyes, take out some paper and write a letter from that Explorer, the future you. In this letter, let the future you share their explorations and wisdom with the present day you.

Chapter 9

Emotions Run Deep

"Healing takes courage, and we all have courage, even if we have to dig a little to find it."

Tori Amos

Ignoring negative feelings such as sadness, frustration and anger, and pretending they don't exist means that you're not dealing with your emotions properly. You're simply stuffing them away inside, where they are likely to fester. Emotional pain from the past takes energy to maintain. It's like trying to keep beach balls underwater. We use up a lot of energy in keeping these emotions below the surface.

Scientists (including James L Oschman PhD, Elliot Drucker MD, Joseph E LeDoux, Ernest L Rossi PhD, Candace B Pert and Deepak Chopra) have discovered that our unacknowledged negative feelings that are not dealt with appropriately reside within the cells of our bodies. These negative emotions can pass from one cellular generation to the next. When negativity is passed on through the cells, part of the cells' vitality shuts down. These areas are where physical or mental illness can occur. When I studied with Brandon Bays and learned The Journey process, she explained that she had actively cleared her cells from negative feelings and recovered from a massive tumour. This process helped to access those repressed cellular memories, clear out the negativity so that vitality can be restored and cells can replicate free from the negativity.

Our cells replicate at an amazing rate. Our skin cells regenerate in about three weeks, liver cells take six weeks, stomach lining only takes three days, and the cells in your eyes renew in less than 48 hours! In just over a year, all the cells in your body have refreshed themselves. Cellularly, you are completely new! That means transformation to full health, happiness and expression is possible in a relatively short period of time – probably quicker than you imagine.

When you *go deep*, you uncover the repressed cell memory and release the stored pain, which then allows the cell to regenerate without the old repressed memory. Clearing away unresolved emotional upsets from your past experiences will result in you having more energy to enjoy the good events in your life. When you clear out emotional dis-ease in your cells, you are also reducing the likelihood of physical dis-ease affecting that area too.

 First Approach: Creating a Safe Space

The tools that follow act as outlets for your feelings, which in turn leads to a shift in your energy. By clearing out the negative feelings in your cells, you allow more room for positive feelings. There are a few approaches that you may find useful. All are about providing an avenue for the suppressed feelings to be expressed.

Using our first approach — creating an environment to express the voice of your young self — let's work on a core negative belief that you uncovered with a previous exercise.

Begin by creating a nurturing space. Choose a room where you can be quiet and without disturbances. Turn off all mobiles and other devices. Allow 45 minutes for each of these exercises.

Imagine the younger you, sitting down beside you. Create a place of comfort for the younger you. Invite the younger you to imagine where that core negative belief is stored in their body. Ask them to describe what that body area looks like.

With the core negative belief in your awareness, bring back into the room the person who was involved with setting up this belief. This could be a parent, a sibling, or a friend, for instance. In my case, I would bring in my father, who would sit across the room from me.

Picture the scene of the younger you sitting beside the present day you and across the room is the person who caused you to create the core negative belief with which you are working.

Core negative beliefs are put in place as a result of unresolved hurts and emotional pain. By setting up this scene for the younger you, you are creating a space for the younger you to be heard.

By speaking from this previous pain, allow the younger you to speak directly to the person who upset them. (The goal here is to clear out any old pains or hurts that the younger you is holding on to and validate the feelings of the younger you).

 ## Second Approach: Three-Stage Exploration

Another way is to express your upset or hurt through a letter that will *never* be sent. Again, it's not about whether the perpetrator is made aware of what happened; it's an outlet for the negative feelings you have buried somewhere inside of you.

With this tool, you are expressing your upset and there are a few stages to it.

Stage 1: Write a letter to the person you feel has hurt or upset you. This person may even be yourself! Just work on one person at a time so you can really focus in on the work. This can be effective with a recent event or something that happened a long time ago.

For this first stage, write what happened and how it made you feel. Write from the emotion that you felt at the time of the hurt. This can be anger, frustration, or any other feeling.

Do not hold back with this letter. You can threaten them and call them the vilest names. Here are a few statements to start you off:

I am angry/frustrated that...

I feel hurt because...

Keep writing without filtering your words. Stay in the emotion. If it's anger you are feeling, write from the anger. When that emotion subsides, there may be tears. Let the tears come.

The next day, check in to see if you have any residual negative emotion around this person in relation to this issue. If you have, repeat the Stage 1 letter-writing exercise. If you need to revisit this stage a few times, so be it. Do not rush through this stage. To truly let go, plan to write these letters as often as is required so as you can clear these unresolved emotional issues.

At the end of this first stage, take note of the following:

I am blaming this person for...................... (how they made you feel)

I have perceived them to have the following opinion/judgment of me (add your belief) ....

Based on this experience/event, I feel........................ towards myself.

To continue with this work, check out the first section of the Strategies chapter.

Third Approach: Action the Anger

Anger loves action! Try one of the following activities while carrying out this exercise. (It will involve shouting, maybe even screaming, so be sure that you can't be overheard or disturbed during this time). Here are some ideas that have worked for my clients:

Running/walking at a brisk pace.

Kneeling over a sofa and hitting the cushion with a tennis racquet.

Shouting into a pillow.

There are other ways that may suit your situation better. This approach is highly effective for some, though not suited to everyone. Whatever way you choose, here are the steps to help you clear that unresolved emotion.

Take a few moments to connect to the unresolved emotion of anger. Revisit the incident that made you feel angry. Welcome all the anger you feel in relation to this incident. Then from that anger, direct your words towards the person involved.

Tell them how they made you feel.

The unfairness of it.

Call them the vilest of names...

The goal here is to allow the suppressed anger to exit your body by focusing it on the person responsible for making you feel angry.

When you have 'emptied out' all the negative feelings, continue the activity. This time, say how that person should have treated you. For instance, say they should have shown you kindness, sensitivity, or patience. By stating these, you are replacing the earlier negative feelings with positive statements, acknowledging your needs.

Stop the activity and take a few moments to settle in with the positive statements of how they should have treated you.

Give yourself practical steps of how you can give this positive feeling to yourself. For instance, if it's kindness, you could say, "I choose to view my work though kind eyes by accepting that I do the best that I can, by complimenting my actions, and by encouraging my progress."

For any feelings or judgments that appear, allow 10 minutes for Ho'oponopono work, which you will also find in the Strategies chapter. When we mentally repeat the Ho'oponopono cleansing tools, we are letting go of judgment and negative feelings around an issue.

We cannot control other people, their actions or their words, but we can control how we respond to them. These tools allow profound healing to take place. As you shift your energy, the energy of the other person changes too. Healing will take place for you both when you forgive.

As Oprah Winfrey says, "True forgiveness is when you can say, 'Thank you for that experience.'" By acknowledging and clearing out the negative emotion, the energy shifts and becomes lighter, more positive and more supportive of you.

Chapter 10

Connection and Communication

"I define connection as the energy that exists between people when they feel seen, heard, and valued; when they can give and receive without judgment; and when they derive sustenance and strength from the relationship."

Brené Brown

Have you ever been hurt? When I ask you this, what responses come to your mind? Did you think of a time when you lost a loved one, or even when someone said something cruel to you? Was your hurt or pain emotional or did you recall a time when you cut a finger or broke a bone or felt physical pain of some kind?

When I ask myself this question, emotional hurt is what I feel first. Instantly. I can almost relive it. The physical pain of burning my arm when lifting a dish out of the oven; that pain is not as 'painful' as the emotional pain of being sad, let down or ignored. Emotional pain is as painful, if not *more* painful than physical pain. We can recall emotional pain when we have unresolved emotional issues or where we have a strong emotional reaction to an event.

Usually, this is a disconnect from another person. We are social creatures. We thrive on connection to others. When that connection is broken, our pain is real and can last a long time — well after the 'loss' occurred.

I listened to a TED talk by Johann Hari on addiction. He spoke of an experiment carried out in the 1970s by psychologists at Simon Fraser University in British Columbia. That experiment showed that rats in isolation overdosed and many even killed themselves by choosing water laced with opium over regular water. Later, a Canadian science team led by Bruce K Alexander built an idyllic setting for rats, which was an inviting, socially rich environment for the animals. Full of activities, other rats, food and again the two bottles of liquid — regular water and water laced with opium. The researchers found that these rats did not typically become addicted to opium or overdose. In fact, they took far less of the drug. The implication is that 'the real cause of addiction' is social isolation.

Our nature is to bond. As humans, we have a natural and innate need to do this. When we are happy and healthy, we fulfil that need to bond. However, if we are isolated, or going through a low time, we may be less likely to connect with other people. And when we are more stressed and have less time to connect in person, we may bond with other substitutes in order to get that happiness hit, contentment or relief.

When people become addicts, they are pushed out to the fringes of society and may even end up in prison. We effectively put up barriers and lessen the likelihood of them being able to reconnect. Hari goes on to explain an approach that Portugal adopted in 2000 to decriminalise all drugs. They also invested money into helping the addicts reconnect with society. Along with regular rehab centres, they put together a massive job creation program. The goal was to make sure that every addict connected back into society and had a reason to get up in the morning. Drug addiction in Portugal is hugely on the decrease and the initiative is hailed as a phenomenal success.

I was reminded of this 'need to connect' quite recently. There was a knock on our front door and Callum went to answer it. He came in to me a little bit puzzled, saying that there was an elderly gentleman looking for Luca, our eldest son. Luca wasn't home so I went out to tell the man. He was a frail man who used a frame to walk. He explained that he had called in a couple of times, but there was no one home. I still was none the wiser as to why he was looking for Luca. And then he said 'I wanted to come over and thank Luca for helping me last week'. I still didn't know what he was talking about. Luca hadn't mentioned anything to me. He went on to explain that the previous week, he had been trying to walk up the road when he felt weak. He had leaned on the wall for some support. When Luca saw him struggling, he helped him.

It was a simple act, so small that Luca had not even mentioned it to me. But here was this man, who was so thankful for that act of kindness, for someone seeing him and taking a moment to connect with him. I was happy and proud that my son had taken this step. It reinforced for me the importance of connection. There are people in our town who are struggling to make those connections, people we won't always see because our faces are in our phones, people who would benefit from a helping hand, a smile or a cuppa with you.

The sheer number of people on Facebook and other social networks illustrates that many people have an intrinsic desire to connect, share and debate with both people they know and relative or complete strangers. I was recently at a public speaking event 'We Can and We Will' held by dynamic Amanda Delaney, someone I'd 'met' through Facebook. Frequently, Amanda would come into my daily life with a comment, a video or a reply to someone else's post. I got to know her that way. So, when she organised this event, I decided to turn up. I felt I already knew her through our interactions on Facebook. At that event, another lady came up to me and said, 'I know you'. We had never met before, though were also friends on Facebook. Today, we can become 'friends' with virtually anyone online, yet when we meet face to face and have that connection, this really can make our hearts sing!

We seem so 'connected' to other people through technology, but are we really connecting? Chatting online via your phone is easier than catching up in person, but is it impeding our capacity to have real and meaningful conversations face to face? Are we losing the art of conversation with the use of smartphones?

Now, I, for one, wouldn't be without my phone. I use it for work like a mobile office, and I use it to connect with family and friends. Though sometimes it reminds me of a primitive roadmap, something we put in place to assist us, but sometimes it actually just gets in the way of real progress. Always remember, it is just a tool. It can never replace face-to-face connection.

In my clinic, I help couples navigate through their differences. Many couples' challenges are rooted in being misunderstood. Although a couple may appear to be arguing over a current issue, that is only part of the story. In our interactions, the majority of arguments are 20% about some current issue and 80% about past unresolved hurts. I call this the 80/20 rule. When your partner pushes your buttons, they are reminding you of past hurts. You hear the imprint of that painful time as part of your old mapping system. When you *go deep*, you can clear out issues that are affecting current relationships.

I remember arriving back home after working in Dublin one time. Our kids were quite small and Fran was working from home. I came in the door, tired, and was met by Fran ranting about something that had happened with the kids. I was about to launch into how tired I was, and the busy few days I'd had in clinic in Dublin, but I decided to take a different route. I knew that being 'right' was not necessarily being 'kind' and I needed to be kind, so I asked Fran to tell me all about it in the clinic room at home.

Let me explain the theory behind the approach I am going to share with you. There is an art to this complicated form of communication... And I'd like to start with where it can go wrong.

When we are hurt or misunderstood, we have two choices:

- Withdraw; or
- Enquire...

To be successful, we need to enter every conversation assuming we have something to learn. Well-known author and famed psychiatrist M Scott Peck said in his book *The Road Less Travelled*, "True listening requires the setting aside of oneself." This 'setting aside' of the self and all its opinions, causes, beliefs and biases is one of the cornerstones of great conversations. It's the courage to *go deep* with the person you are speaking to.

There are a few key tips I will share here on how to do this.

1. Park your emotions. Put them on the shelf until you are able to deal with it properly. If you are in an emotional state, this is not the time to have the conversation... Wait! Then when you are ready to have the conversation, come from a place of curiosity.
2. Have the end in sight. What is it you want to achieve in this conversation?
3. Be patient and listen. Slow the conversation down and truly listen. We all like to be heard, to be really heard. The person you are engaging with may well have insights you hadn't counted on.

Active Listening

So, what happened in my example? Well, there and then, we went into the clinic room and I took the 'active listening' approach. This is an effective tool that I give to clients too. During active listening, the listener listens intently. The listener parks their own 'story' on the shelf and listens. Every so often, the listener repeats back to the speaker what they have heard; this is for clarification that what the listener heard is actually what the speaker meant to say. It also shows the speaker that the listener was truly listening.

I did this with Fran and truly listened to him. He started off by ranting a little about the kids and the usual goings on with young children. I knew there had to be more. Fran is so intuitive and patient with the children, and they absolutely adore him, so I stayed listening and empathised with him. One of the children had said something to him and it opened an old wound he had about his own father. I listened some more... Finally, Fran said, 'This is nothing to do with the kids. This is about something my dad said to me once'.

In the end, it turned out Fran's reaction was more about something that had happened in the past than what had happened that day. We hugged it out as is the norm in our family and Fran could take that insight into an old pattern and use it for healing. If I had not listened, he would not have had the opportunity to uncover this old pattern. I really did very little. I just validated his feelings and gave him the space to work through the 80/20 scenario.

Clear communication is a window into the world of your partner; truly being heard and understood is easily achievable with the right tools. We all have our own primitive roadmaps. We all have emotional baggage from that. And we all need to be validated and heard. This is not only in relationships with your partner, but also with your children, your friends, and your work colleagues. On the other side, we can all be that listening ear for the people in our lives.

By communicating, we exchange information and its meaning, right? Or do we? "The single biggest problem in communication is the illusion that is has taken place" is a quote attributed to George Bernard Shaw that is relevant here. Conversations can be tricky. Have you ever had a meeting with your colleagues only to realise they took away from it a different understanding than you did? Or spoken with your partner and later realised that their interpretation (or memory) of that conversation is very different to yours? What causes this to take place? During a conversation, the words that we hear and their meanings are passed through our roadmap, our individual mapping system. As we know, this is made up of our strongly held opinions, beliefs and attitudes, which have been shaped and reinforced over a lifetime. We all have different perceptions based on our individual mapping system and we can interpret events differently, though we all feel we are right! Now you can see how we interpret the same event differently!

It seems one of the most common outcomes of communication is misunderstanding. Being misunderstood happens frequently. Think of how much energy you expend on pointless arguments over misunderstandings! To enhance your relationship with another person, get to know their mapping system. You can then understand how they view the world, which reduces misunderstandings.

WOW in Your Relationships

Here is an exercise you can use to help resolve a misunderstanding. Take a few moments to consider the following, let's enquire with the WOW of conversations.

What happened: Without an overlay of our assumptions, what happened and how does that make you feel? Who else is it affecting – other family members or perhaps work colleagues?

Own it: How might you have contributed to this situation? Is there something you did/did not say or do?

Win it: What outcome would be beneficial to you and the other person?

When it's resolved, what positive implications will it have for you, the other person and/or others who may be impacted by this?

How does it make you feel?

Who else will benefit from this resolution?

Having had this WOW conversation with yourself, it's time to resolve this with the other person. First, let them know in advance what your intention is. Let them know that you are aware of the misunderstanding and would like to work on resolving it.

When does it suit them?

By changing our approach to conversations, we can reduce misunderstanding and deepen our level of understanding, which improves how we connect, communicate and collaborate. In his book *The 7 Habits of Highly Effective People*, Stephen Covey says it beautifully, "Most people do not listen with the intent to understand; they listen with the intent to reply." Traditional conversations tend to be defined by what we tell rather than by what we ask. Yet all my coaching experience has taught me that what builds a relationship, what solves problems and what moves situations forward is asking the right questions. Building new relationships can be enhanced when we adopt *The ABC of Conversations*, which is the next tool I would like to share with you and is based on conversations in general.

*A*sking questions to which you may not already know the answer;

*B*uilding a relationship based on curiosity and interest in the other person; and

*C*larifying so as you understand what is being said.

Enter each conversation with the openness that 'everyone has something to teach me'. If you can find it within yourself to stop using conversations to convince people that you're right, you will be stunned at what you've been missing.

There will be times, and no doubt we have all experienced it, when we have been on the receiving end of someone misinterpreting our words. How many times have we said 'that's not what I meant' because a friend or family member has taken our words up wrong? I have worked with many teams and committees, which can be challenging for the same reason. Everyone is passionate about the task, everyone has their own approach and somehow you need to harness their enthusiasm, celebrate their differences and sustain a team spirit.

Courageous Conversations

I suggest looking at all your relationships, individual and team, business and personal, where there has been a breakdown in communication. Adopt these approaches and see if you can get those relationships back on track. Also, in your community, consider striking up a conversation with someone that you haven't connected with before. Make that connection, ask questions and build relationships.

I have brought my 'courageous conversations' to teams in both the workplace and in community groups. To see a group transform, when you equip them with effective communication skills and allow them to be courageous in their conversations, is truly an awesome experience.

As social creatures, we thrive on connection to others. Yet those relationships can be hindered by old roadmaps as our different perceptions can lead to miscommunication. To enhance those relationships, pop on your Explorer cap, investigate your own core beliefs and clear out those that don't serve you. Uncover your hidden treasures and you will deepen those vital connections.

Chapter 11

Take Your Parachutes and Jump!

"Always remember that your present situation is not your final destination, the best is yet to come."

Zig Ziglar

We all have times in our life when people have a negative impact on us, people who can erode our confidence and potential. And then there are times when people have a positive impact on us, people who support us, lift us up, like a *parachute*. Sometimes without us even realising it at the time.

Born in 1942, Charles Plumb was raised in rural Kansas City. He grew up on a farm with no indoor plumbing until he was 11 years old. In 1956, his family moved to Overland Park, a Kansas City suburb. Charles loved planes and dreamed of one day flying one. He graduated from the U.S. Naval Academy and was awarded his Navy Wings of Gold in 1966. He reported to Miramar Naval Air Station in San Diego where he flew the first adversarial flights in the development of what would come to be called the Navy Fighter Weapons School, currently known as TOPGUN.

The next year, Plumb's squadron, the Aardvarks, launched on the aircraft Kittyhawk to fly the Navy's airplane, the F-4 Phantom Jet. Charles Plumb flew 74 successful combat missions over Vietnam. On his 75th mission, with just five days before he was to return home, his plane was shot down over Hanoi, by a surface to air missile. Plumb parachuted into enemy territory, where he was captured and tortured. He spent the next 2,103 days in an 8x8 foot cell, as a prisoner of war in North Vietnam.

He survived the ordeal and now lectures on lessons learned from the experience. One day, when Plumb and his wife were sitting in a restaurant, a man at another table came up and said, "You're Plumb! You flew jet fighters in Vietnam from the aircraft carrier Kittyhawk. You were shot down!" "How in the world did you know that?" asked Plumb. "I packed your parachute," the man replied. Plumb gasped in surprise and gratitude. The man pumped his hand and said, "I guess it worked!" Plumb assured him, "It sure did, if your 'chute hadn't worked, I wouldn't be here today."

Plumb recalled that he couldn't sleep that night, thinking about that man. Of the experience, he said, "I kept wondering what he might have looked like in a Navy uniform — a Dixie cup hat, a bib in the back, and bell-bottom trousers. I wondered how many times I might have passed him on the Kittyhawk. I wondered how many times I might have seen him and not even said, "Good morning, how are you?" or anything, because I was a fighter pilot and he was 'just a sailor'." Plumb thought of the many hours the sailor had spent on a long wooden table in the bowels of the ship carefully weaving the shrouds and folding the silks of each parachute, holding in his hands each time the fate of someone he didn't know.

Plumb also points out that he needed many kinds of *parachutes* when his plane was shot down over enemy territory. He needed his physical *parachute*, his mental *parachute*, his emotional *parachute*, and his spiritual *parachute*.

Who's Packing Your Parachute?

When I heard that story, it reminded me of all the amazing *parachutes* I have had throughout my life. Have you ever thought what these are for you? Who provides your safety nets of emotional support, physical support, and mental support? Who has made an everlasting impression? These may well be the unsung heroes in your life!

When I was young, I had two amazing *parachutes* who I was fortunate to spend a lot of time with. They were my refuge. I grew up in a typical housing estate on the southside of Dublin. There were children around my age in the estate and shops within walking distance, but like so many housing estates built in the 1950s, little thought was given to amenities for young people. We had a big field in the shape of a semi-circle, which was flanked by a laneway around the arched side and a road opposite. We also had a gem of a man on that estate.

If you turned right out of my garden gate and walked to the end of the road, which was only four houses away, there was a corner house with a large wall. Opposite that was Mr. O'Byrne's house. Everyone called him Mr. O. His house was one of the houses that backed onto the laneway at the field. He had five children, his youngest lad being my age. This was not what made him a gem, though. His priceless quality was in what he did for us kids...

A quiet, unassuming, small-framed man, when he finished his day's work at 3pm, he would turn his mere 10ftx12ft garage into our community centre! Health and safety regulations were not an issue back then. And thankfully so! His garage was a gathering place for children between the ages of seven and seventeen. There was always something happening in The Garage. A table tennis table would occupy it one day as we would all wait our turn. This could then easily be put on its side and pushed against the wall to make way for other activities. One summer, he got the older kids to paint the inside of his garage. Not your traditional type of painting. The base colour was a bright blue and it was adorned with every kid's foot and hand print in the colours of the rainbow!

At weekends, complete with disco ball and lights, we would have Bob's Disco, one to rival any 'real' disco in the area. The evening was divided into two halves. The younger kids below the age of twelve had the floor until 8:30pm and afterwards the older kids had it until 10.30pm. This was in the days when dance routines were all the rage. We would be busy during the week putting the finishing touches to our performance. "Night Fever" by the Bee Gees was a favourite! Then we'd turn up to The Garage, all dressed up in matching dresses, and feel like disco queens. When our requested song was played, we would take to the dance floor. It was the best!

Sunday mornings were not off-limits either. A group of six or more kids would all sit on the wall opposite Mr. O's and wait for him to drop off Mrs. O after Mass. We would then *all* pile into his silver Ford Escort and be transported up to the swimming pool in Templeogue College.

During the summer holidays, we would all go en masse to Mr. O's, where he would fill our days with games in the field. Games like football, rounders and track events, culminating in a sports day for us all. On sunny afternoons, we would regularly pile into his trusty car, two persons deep, and he would take us on a country run. His trips would take in places like the Meeting of the Waters and Glendalough. The highlight of the summer was the organised trip on a double decker bus to Butlin's which Mr. O' would organise.

His little garage was bursting at the seams and Mr. O' organised to have an extension built. It was a humble room just big enough to house his armchair, a little fireplace and a table around which we could squeeze four to six people. This was a hub of activity. He taught us how to play the card game Don, which would fill many a winter's night. Or for a change, he would take out an extra-large jigsaw puzzle and that would keep us all entertained. Mr. O' would sit there, smoking his pipe - never judging, always accepting.

When I think back to how he gave so much to us kids, I recognise Mr. O' as this calming presence. I would visit Mr. O's garage from around the age of 10 until I was about 15. It was an oasis. And so relaxing being around his calm demeanour. He uplifted me, when I felt I was falling.

He was my *parachute*.

Grandad O'Donnell lived just two minutes up the road from us. He suffered a stroke when I was quite young and my aunties and uncle cared for him. One of my aunties, Vera, would care for him in the evenings and weekends. Vera was a nun who taught primary school children. I frequently stayed with her at weekends. I am not very creative, however any creativity I may possess is all down to Auntie Vera. She would teach me how to sew teddies and cushions. These Teddies came in a variety of colours and her cushion pattern involved some delicate sowing. I loved the challenge and I particularly loved spending time with Vera. She was always so patient and generous with her time. We would sit for hours just creating and enjoying each others company.

She was my *parachute*.

With Vera and Mr. O', I got to be safe outside my family home. They were my serenity. I have been blessed with many *parachutes* in my life, whose kind words, acceptance and calming influence cut through the inner turmoil I was feeling. With them in my corner, I felt I could do anything. They gave me support — emotional support — and with that, I could glide gently back to earth with a strength to try new things.

 Fieldwork:

Look for people who inspire you. You don't even have to meet them or know them personally. You can find them on the internet, on TED talks, through seminars or in books. Surround yourself with people who build you up, who encourage you and also challenge you.

Who are your *parachutes*? Who supports you?

What kind words or actions have had a positive influence on you?

Who can you offer this kind of support to in your life? Who can you influence in a positive way? Who will you be a *parachute* for?

Chapter 12

Be Open to Engage

"Every problem has in it the seeds of its own solution. If you don't have any problems, you don't get any seeds."

Norman Vincent Peale

Your altitude is determined by your attitude. People around you can influence your attitude. Have you found that? Has anyone ever impacted you and changed your mood? I have loosely grouped people into the following groups to categorise their influence on the attitudes of others around them - radiators, drainers and polluters.

Radiators are people who radiate good vibes and have a positive attitude. We have all been in the company of people who are uplifting, positive and encouraging. They enter a room and there is a warmth about them. These people have a positive impact on us. I was having an ongoing issue with a woman I worked with in one of my first jobs. This woman's passive aggression was really getting me down. I wanted to tell someone. I knew telling one friend would result in her having a 'pity party' with me and I realised that that would disempower me even more. I would feel more of a victim. I decided to turn to two other friends and confide in them. Why? I knew they would listen, as the first friend would, but that they would then sit with me and help me come up with workable solutions and ways of moving forward. Radiators are solution-focused and don't engage in pity parties. I have amazing friends and it's easy to have a positive attitude around these people.

Then there are the *drainers*. When they enter the room, these people always seem to need a pep talk, and tend to drain you of some positivity. It's not so easy to have a good attitude around these people. I must admit, there have been times when I have been a drainer, when I wasn't in top form or even near it. There have been times when I seemed 'stuck' and could only see the negative in a person or an issue. Have you ever just been fed up listening to yourself moaning about something? I soon realised that when I am stuck in the draining cycle, there is something that needs to shift. This is an invitation to *go deep* and clear out some belief that I am running.

We then have the *polluters*. Unfortunately, these people will always see the cup as being half empty. The navigation system of these people creates quite a negative interpretation of their surroundings. These include the gossipers, people who put others down and the ones who resent other people's achievements. They have the potential of polluting your mood and it's worth considering whether you really need them in your personal life. They have their advantages. In business, in particular, they may help sharpen your skills. These people can build your mental toughness. However, they can be detrimental to your self-confidence. These are the doubters, the cynics and those who throw negativity and critical comments your way. These people could benefit from *going deep*. Do you know any polluters?

Choosing How You Respond

How do you react to rudeness, anger, or sarcasm? How do you respond to a slow, rude waitress? How do you respond to a traffic delay or a cold dreary day? When someone gives you an undeserved blast of their horn, do you blast right back?

I had a recent encounter with a rude waitress. She was gruff in her approach to me, slow, and not very pleasant. I began to take exception to this and made some comment to my friend who was with me about the waitress's attitude. Then I saw my STOP sign! I was starting to let this waitress affect my time out with my friend. Could this be perceived differently? Perhaps, the waitress was having a bad day at work. Perhaps, her boss was angry and had taken his anger out on her. Perhaps, she had challenges at home. Whatever her reason for her rude behaviour, I knew I had nothing to do with it. In other words, it wasn't about me and I was not going to take it personally.

Do you let others pull you down to their level or do you recognise that the incident probably has *nothing* to do with you? Someone may have just experienced an upset in their day. You just happened to be the next one in line and their behaviour has nothing to do with you.

Your response to people will largely determine your success and happiness in life. You may not be able to control how others behave; however, you can control how you choose to respond to their behaviour. You cannot control people's actions, but you have **complete control** over your reactions.

Robert Schuller, a world-renowned motivational speaker, differentiates between an optimist and a pessimist like this: "The pessimist says, 'I'll believe it when I see it', whereas the optimist says, 'I'll see it when I believe it'." The optimist takes action; the pessimist takes a seat.

Your attitude is how you respond to ideas, people or situations, and it is the greatest force in your life. It's a power that is also yours to define. If you decide to have a positive one, you increase your personal power exponentially. Attitude influences your choice of action and responses to challenges, incentives and rewards!

Inner beliefs we have about ourselves will determine how we respond to life, but anyone has the potential of making an emotional impact on us. If you want to catch the right mental attitude, go where that attitude exists. Which group of people would you like to be around? Who would you seek advice from? Who will help you thrive? Who is currently influencing you? Motivational speaker Jim Rohn says, "We are the average of the five people we spend the most time with", so start by looking there.

How do we get and then keep the right mental attitude regardless of outside conditions, people, weather, etc? First, go to the people who have the right mental attitude. Get a mentor, work with a coach, start reading more of the right books, listen to more of the right podcasts or watch the right videos. These are your *parachutes*!

I remember attending a seminar on positive mental attitude when I was about 20 years old. I came out oozing positivity. I was going to change the world! Yet the following Monday, I returned to my job. A week later, I was feeling far from positive. I got frustrated, dropped around to see Mr. O, and told him that I had tried this positive attitude approach and it wasn't working. "I went to a seminar last week, but I feel worse today than before I went", I explained. Mr. O said he was reminded of a story he'd heard from Zig Ziglar. "Karen, did you have dinner today?" he asked. "I did, but what has that got to do with achieving my dreams?" I replied. Mr. O continued, "Do you plan on eating tomorrow, Karen?" "Of course, I do", I replied. He went on, "Karen, if you ate yesterday, why do you need to eat again today and then again tomorrow?"

I could see where he was going with this. Our minds have the potential to reach our goals. To achieve happiness, we need to feed them often.

What is your mental appetite like? When was the last time you deliberately, on a predetermined schedule, fed your mind good food? The positivity with which you feed your mind can create effective and supportive *parachutes*. You can feed your mind using external means but also internal methods.

I will consider internal *parachutes* in the next chapter, but for the remainder of this chapter, let's focus on the *parachutes* you can access externally.

External Parachutes

I have invested thousands of hours and euros in developing my *parachutes* externally. The world is full of drainers and polluters, and surrounding yourself with radiators is vital for any progress in life, personal or business.

At times, I have been that polluter or drainer myself, when I felt a victim, or had a pity party for the way life was or wasn't turning out. At times, I would put the blame firmly on other people's shoulders. It was someone else's fault that I didn't achieve X, Y or Z. However, I learned that as long as I was blaming others, I was letting them control *my* future. Whereas, if I took responsibility, I was empowering *me*.

Blame and judgement, in my opinion, are two of the biggest roadblocks on our maps. When you remove them, it's amazing how you gain ground quickly and efficiently. Once you own that responsibility, you take back the driving seat of your life. You regain the ability to respond to your circumstances. Maintaining that positive responsiveness is very much improved with the help of *parachutes.*

Parachutes come in a several varieties:-

Mentors

I have been extremely fortunate to find mentors who provided the knowledge, wisdom and encouragement I needed to flourish. Mentors see the potential in their mentee, usually long before the mentee is aware it exists!

If you find a good mentor, hold on tight. It can be a very rewarding relationship. In any area of life when you want to stretch outside of your comfort zone, when you want to take that leap of faith, it's much easier when you can be supported by a mentor who will help you navigate to your destination.

I have had the privilege of mentoring some amazing people. As a mentor, I am committed to helping my mentees find success by empowering them to develop their own strengths, beliefs and personal attributes.

Mastermind groups

A mastermind group can be made up of two or more people with different attributes, who can support and motivate each person in the group. Mastermind groups offer a combination of brainstorming, education, support and sometimes peer accountability.

I am involved with several mastermind groups. Here, I get to learn from other people. Members challenge one another to set strong though realistic goals and encourage one another to accomplish them. When I am stretching outside of my comfort zone, I know this will yield the quickest learning for me and is more easily done with a group of supportive leaders cheering me on from the side-lines.

By creating goals, designing a plan and working towards achieving it, you can share successes and gain advice on overcoming challenges. I love brainstorming with different people in the group as the adage 'two heads are better than one' rings true. With 10 heads, you just never know what hair-brained suggestions will come up and lead to creating concrete plans. Strong facilitators can be the magic behind a thriving mastermind group.

Accountability buddies

If you have a mastermind group, you may have an accountability buddy that you can connect with. Having a business associate who will hold you accountable and gently support you in this way is invaluable. An accountability buddy offers guidance and holds you to your commitments. Avoid having a friend or family member to be your accountability buddy as they may be too close to you emotionally and may 'let you off the hook'. An accountability buddy can also be working towards their own goals. If they are working towards similar goals to yourself, it gives you both a frame of reference.

Cheerleaders

I get great pleasure in supporting others' progress. Whether this is with clients on a personal level or in business, we can all be *parachutes* for one another. Both giving and receiving of support can be instrumental in achieving and maintaining a positive attitude.

In my case, my cheerleaders are my family, my friends and also my group of mastermind buddies.

Books

Such an accessible way to get positive and uplifting food for your mind, who doesn't love to flick through a book and be carried away by the words dancing on the page?

From my childhood, I would hop on a bus to Eason's every Saturday. I would spend hours in their bookstore on O'Connell Street in Dublin. I loved horses and would work my way through their vast selection of books. My teacher in 5th and 6th class, Mrs. Kennedy, nurtured my love of reading. She would read to us every afternoon, before home time, and would encourage us all to read a book from her private library in the classroom. Back then, I loved to lose myself in the stories. I always remember her reading *The Wind in the Willows*. She had such a beautiful voice. In her classroom library, she also had a dog eared copy of *Watership Down* by Richard Adams. I read it from cover to cover in just a few days. Although considered a children's book, it was so inspiring. It may have been a story about rabbits, but it was also a tale of kindness, inspiration and motivation.

Towards the end of my teenage years, I began reading inspirational and motivational books. Some of my favourite books are Zig Ziglar's *See You At The Top*, Og Mandino's *The Gift of Acabar*, M. Scott Peck's *The Road Less Travelled* and Susan Jeffers' *Feel The Fear and Do It Anyway*. Many explosions went off in my mind when I would explore these books.

When I talk with people about books, it amazes me that some people think that they do not 'need' to read or listen to inspirational or motivational material unless they are feeling down. I do get their point. When you are feeling down, the *need* is more obvious. You want a book that uplifts you and helps you find your way back up to the lighter feelings. The right book can do that for you. When you are already emotionally *up* and moving, you could utilise all that energy to really propel yourself forward. When you are *down*, you tend to be problem-focused, whereas when you are *up* and moving forward, it can fuel your optimism and ambition. You are solution-focused instead of problem-focused. That's when you will raise your performance. Your attitude and enthusiasm will increase. You'll achieve results.

Information is a lot more accessible now. We can find motivation online. We can google it. We can access books through various devices. Buy online versions and they appear on your device immediately. We can explore books by reading or listening. We can take our exploring into the car, by listening to podcasts or books on audio. We can keep connected to all these supportive *parachutes* even when we are on the go.

I regularly drive long distances for work and use this time as my university of life on wheels. I take these opportunities to get a shot of positivity via podcasts or audiobooks. Some of my favourites to listen to in the car would be Joe Vitale, Wayne Dyer and of course Zig Ziglar. Sometimes I just throw in some good old-fashioned music. Something upbeat with a rock anthem might do the trick. Something Happens' song "Parachute" is apt here, so "take your parachute and jump!"

Events

There is nothing like connecting with like-minded people in person, though. I attended my first personal growth seminars towards the end of my teenage years, though it wasn't until I was in my thirties when I began to go more regularly. Interactive workshops are my favourite where I can try out the advice in practice. This is the format I use when I am giving workshops. It's important for me that attendees have an experiential time at my workshops and can immediately see the value of it. They soak in the supportive positive atmosphere, feel the shifts and go home with lots of transformational tools.

All in all, a parachute is no good unless it's used. Having one strapped to your back when you take that leap of faith is useless if you're not willing to open and engage it. Make it a priority to take a leap with the assistance of a mentor, explore many other books, and drop in on a seminar! "Your *parachute* won't let you down", so the song goes. This will keep you inspired, motivated and solution-focused, raising your performance in how you show up in your life, either personally or in business. Your attitude, enthusiasm and positivity will increase, and you will actively make progress towards your dreams.

Chapter 13

If It's Going To Be, It's Up To Me!

"Don't let the noise of others' opinions drown out your own inner voice."

Steve Jobs

While discussing the importance of **parachutes**, I have suggested many external ways of support. However, the type of **parachute** that will fundamentally make an enormous impact on where and how you navigate is your inner **parachute**. In other words, what is your attitude towards you?

Have you ever been struck by a 'eureka' moment, when pure inspiration comes to you in the form of a great idea? You feel that internal joy at the wonderful possibilities that can unfold. You see the beautiful plan take shape and you bask in the glory of your amazing ideas. Then your head steps in with all its negative reasons why the idea won't work and reminds you of when you failed in the past!

How many potential successes have been ruined by our inner self-talk? If we are holding a negative thought about ourselves, we can self-sabotage. The good news is we have the power to change it. Remember, the greatest force in our lives is our attitude! It's a personal power that is yours to define.

If you decide it will be positive, you increase your personal power exponentially.

This self-sabotaging used to happen to me frequently. At times, even now, it tries to creep in. However, as I now have a variety of effective tools, I laugh at the mind games and move forward.

Internal Parachutes

In order to change your results and become your own best supporter, you must change your beliefs about yourself. You may hold a belief that 'nothing good happens to me'. Whatever the thought, enquire of yourself, 'Is this true?' When you put your Explorer hat on, you will find evidence in your past to verify that good things have happened to you. Once you *go deep* and clear out the negative programming, *parachutes* are about having more space for positivity and creativity, which you can use to support yourself in the future.

Self-talk

One of the keys to working towards your goals is your self-talk, your internal dialogue. A positive internal dialogue brings you closer to your goals by nurturing a positive belief system about yourself. Master this tool and it will soon be supporting you in all your endeavours.

 Returning to our 'eureka' moment, just as we have a brilliant idea, the mind steps in to point out when we have failed in the past. Here's how to overcome this:

- See a STOP sign!
- Turn that negative thought 180 degrees and identify the positive thought.
- Create a statement.
- Back it up with evidence, by visualising success.

The opposite of failing is succeeding, so the thought you want to identify is succeeding or being successful. Yet it is not enough just to say, "I am successful". Your mind may well come back with "Oh yeah?" in that questioning way it has a habit of doing. Your mind is based on logic, so it needs facts to back up these statements.

Positive Collage

Your mind loves a job and it loves to prove itself right. Imagine all your data is stored in a filing cabinet in your mind. Give your mind a job. Send it to search the filing cabinet of your life and highlight times when you were successful. Ask it to find three events and see each event play out. See the setting, hear people congratulating you, feel what that felt like to you, see yourself smiling. Get your senses involved in this as much as possible.

One such event may be when you succeeded in riding a bicycle. Picture your parents excitedly taking the stabilisers off; you are holding the handle bars, peddling with all your strength while keeping the bike upright! You pushed on through the fear and you conquered it! *You succeeded* and you felt on the top of the world at four years old. You felt like you could achieve anything!

Put this factual image into a factual positive collage in your mind's eye. Now, what else have you achieved?

Maybe you have an experience of passing your driving test; passing an exam; going out with that boy or girl you always fancied. You can keep adding to your factual positive collage of success.

If, in the future, a negative thought enters your mind, doubting your ability, such as, "You can't do this", or "You can't do that", or "Who do you think you are? That won't work", see the STOP sign. Consider the opposite, "I can do that!" Now, find the evidence and turn it into a positive factual collage of your successes. Obliterate that negative thought!

If you are running common themes in your negative thoughts, start building positive collages now. Actively sit down and start building them. I have drawn up a list of common monkey chatter that may enter my mind — the thoughts that are demeaning to me. An example of one was,

"You can't do that". That voice does wear you down! Voices will tend to appear when you are trying something new and your primitive roadmap doesn't want you to fail. The best way to not fail is to not try! There is a crazy logic to your roadmap, remember.

In these circumstances, I would make up my positive collage. I would visit the various scenes. Then, whenever that monkey chatter tried to put me down or doubt me, I could access my positive memories on my factual positive collage and clear out that inner saboteur.

Let's say you are following directions on a road trip and you take a wrong turn. Your immediate response might be to berate yourself, saying things like, "You always mess up directions". Let's work through this example:

"You always mess up directions."

See the STOP sign! Consider the opposite, "I don't mess up directions!" Now, give your mind a job and pull out the times in your life when you followed directions. Again, it's not enough just to say the positive statement, you need to back it up with facts. Real and specific events.

Make a statement and follow with a factual example:

I followed directions and found Martina's house in Sligo.

I followed directions and found Gary's house in Galway.

I followed directions and found the cinema in Carlow.

You might get back in the driver's seat and say, "On this occasion, I took a wrong turn. However, I frequently get directions right. I got to Martina's house in Sligo, Gary's house in Galway and I found the cinema in Carlow."

In this way, you are stopping the negativity in your head before it has time to potentially ruin your mood and your day.

Doing this engages one of your superpowers, the **reticular activating system** (RAS) of the brain that can, at your will, focus your attention. More on the RAS in the upcoming Strategies section. For now, know that focusing in on your positive traits means you are training your brain to seek out the best in you!

Positive self-talk can create your best *parachute* and that inner support can help you in every situation in life.

Chapter 14

Strategies - Unlocking That Prison Door

"As I walked out the door toward the gate that would lead to my freedom, I knew if I didn't leave my bitterness and hatred behind, I'd still be in prison."

Nelson Mandela

One of the most amazing aspects of being human is that we feel emotions. However, not all the emotions we experience feel positive. We have all been in many different situations throughout our lives where we have experienced events where the emotions that we felt have been painful. For example, we have felt sadness and anger. We may have experienced jealousy, resentment, or unfair treatment by others. Often, the emotional hurt we experienced at that time, we hold onto for several years, sometimes a lifetime.

When you *go deep*, one of the areas we work on is forgiveness. Using my experiences as an example, thoughts of forgiving my father did not sit well with me for several reasons. I didn't want to let him 'off the hook'. I didn't want him 'getting away' with what he had done. I somehow felt that, by holding onto the pain and not forgiving him, he was still suffering. What was really happening, though, was that I was still holding onto the upset of these events, and not allowing myself to heal and move forward.

As you have read, I did decide to forgive my father. When considering this, I faced another dilemma, however. This pain was part of my story. Who was I without my story?

Identity

I had what could be considered a dawning realisation - that my distress was part of my story. If I cleared the associated pain, who was I? Was I holding onto the pain so some crazy identity crisis didn't happen? Could I step outside of the pain, step outside of the shadows that these events cast on my life? Then there came a realisation - that I was 'gaining' something by holding onto these stories. I had an identity. *Wow!* That was an 'aha' moment for me. I had to have a word with myself, and to be fair, it was many words over a long period of time. Part of my identity was having this pain. Part of how I coped in life was as a direct result of this pain. By considering moving forward, I had to look at the impact that any changes could have on me, on my identity.

When you write that out, it looks crazy on the page. Surely any 'normal' person would want to clear out all that anguish, right? Why was I hesitating? Fear had crept in, of course. My mind played games with me. Who would I be without this hurt inside? This hurt was like a comfort blanket. It may not have been a very 'comfortable' comfort blanket, but it was familiar and always there for me. It had never let me down. I could still feel that hurt, after all these years, even though these events were long gone.

Who was keeping that pain alive? Who was keeping that story alive? It was me! Those incidents were well in the past, yet I would bring up the pain and repeatedly hurt *myself* with those memories time and time again. I made choices based on the memories that I continued to carry around with me. Although the physical abuse had been over a long time ago,

I, myself, was continuing the emotional hurt over and over. Wow!

It was a bitter pill to swallow that the story was no longer about my father hurting me, but about *me* hurting me by keeping the story and drama alive.

Forgiveness

Whenever I had thought about forgiveness previously, my knee-jerk reaction was - my forgiveness won't change his actions, so why should I forgive him? There is some truth in that. I couldn't change his actions. Yet forgiveness is not about that. Forgiveness is concerned with our attitude not their action. By changing our attitude, we are taking back the power and releasing 'ourselves' from the pain. Amazing, right? We are growing as a result of forgiving, not remaining victims.

Another factor in my hesitation was that I mistakenly thought I had to tell him to his face that I had forgiven him. However, I wasn't doing it for him; I was doing it for me. For *my* growth. I realised that not only did I need to let this issue go, and move on past it, but I needed to forgive myself as well as my father. When I made that realisation, my mind went into meltdown. I questioned my sanity. Why did I need forgiveness when I was the victim? Why would I want to move on from this story if it helped me make choices that kept me safe? I was afraid to take on opportunities as I was too afraid of the outcomes. I made decisions based on past hurts and that made my world quite small, as I tried to control every event!

I needed to move on from the stories that had created a toxic inner environment. And if forgiving my father and myself allowed me to move on, then forgiveness it was going to have to be!

You have a choice. When you are hurt emotionally, you can choose to hold onto the anger and resentment, standing tall on your moral high ground, *or* you can embrace forgiveness and move on. If, like me, you struggle with forgiveness because you feel you have the right to be angry and the other person does not have the right to your kindness, know that forgiveness will give you the opportunity to heal.

When I finally forgave my father — and it did take several *go deep* sessions — it was like the emotional charge that held these stories was gone. It no longer was painful to recall the stories. They no longer had a hold on me. What I realised was, while I kept resenting my father, I was giving him control over my feelings. However, when I took the steps to forgive him, I was taking the responsibility for moving forward and I was reclaiming that power! I hadn't realised the burden of carrying around those negative feelings and the attached stories. This emotional baggage went everywhere with me. What a lot of energy it took! Once I forgave, the tension and charge evaporated, and I felt free from living under the burden of having to deal with the feelings of this story. I felt enlightened after letting this story go.

Forgiveness is a win-win strategy. It releases you from the pain of past events and lets you move on. Energetically, it releases the other person from the event too.

 Fieldwork:

The following 'forgiveness' tool is a strategy you can learn. Though like anything new, start with easier events and work up to those you find more difficult or painful. One-off events such as a colleague who has let you down will be easier than ongoing events like bullying or other highly charged emotional issues. Those issues are best worked through with a facilitator.

Take 45 minutes for this exercise. Create a quiet space where you won't be disturbed. Turn off mobiles and all other devices. Get lots of paper and a pen. This is a 'writing' exercise. Do not reduce the effect by typing. When doing this writing exercise, work on one person at a time. The person could even be yourself.

This is a recap of Stage 1 that we have already seen in the *Go Deep* section.

 Stage One

Firstly, write a brief description of what happened.

What was the underlying issue?

Here are a few examples:

Were you controlled; attacked verbally; let down; lied to; discriminated against; exploited?

Take a moment to recall this event. Check in with your body and note any emotional charge that is still associated with this event. Walk through the event again and note the feeling that seems to be associated with this story. When you are remembering this, feel how emotional is it for you.

What emotional charge would you place on this upsetting story?

Rate it out of 10. If, when you think about it, you don't get too upset, then give it a low number. If you get upset give it a higher number.

For example, when I recalled the stories from my childhood, it would almost bring me to tears. I would feel the fear and pain as if it was happening to me at that moment. That would get a 10/10. When I recall it now, it's just a story, part of my life's tapestry. I can see so many 'treasures' from this event. I can see all the skills I have developed and my many learnings.

Describe the situation in detail and how you felt about it at the time. Write what happened and how it made you feel. Write about the feelings· hurt, guilt, anger, disappointment, shame, or any other feelings that you felt. Get all your emotions out onto the page without filtering your words. This is *your* opportunity to let out all the emotion you are feeling in relation to this. Do not hold back.

Write from the emotion you are feeling. If you felt humiliated, write from that humiliation. If it's anger, write from that anger. Write *as if you are addressing the person*. Instead of saying, 'X made me feel worthless', write, '*You* made me feel worthless'. Sometimes we might downgrade the emotion to a more socially acceptable form. So, we might sanitise it by saying, 'I am *annoyed* with X' or mute the anger to *sadness*. Try to stay in the active emotion, the emotion you felt at the time of the hurt. Do not let the other person 'off the hook'.

Stage 2: The next day, write from the other person's point of view. When you have written from that emotional place, pause and give yourself time to consider looking at this from the other person's perspective. What may have led them to take that approach, to say those things, to upset you? If the other person did not intend to cause upset or hurt or harm, why might they have done what they did?

Although we don't condone their behaviour, we do try to see it from their perspective. By using this approach, this exercise will illicit some understanding as to why they acted the way they did. Perhaps allow some compassion to develop, along with the possibility of being open to forgiving them for the part they played in this issue. Finish this stage with the following statement:

I am open to looking at this in a different way.

Stage 3: The next day, write about the opportunity for growth that may have presented itself. Aside from the hurt and pain you felt, could this be an opportunity for you to grow? With soft eyes, consider the following:

Could this person be mirroring you in some way?

Have you ever treated yourself like this person has treated you?

Could this be presenting you an opportunity for self-forgiveness?

Another way of approaching this potential for growth is to see if your qualities can be validated.

Has this person not validated your worth?

Have you ever not validated your worth?

Based on the answers you gave in Stage 1, might there be a part of you that also carries these feelings or judgments about yourself or others?

Could this incident be an opportunity for your own spiritual growth?

A step in moving forward is accepting ourselves.

When you have completed these stages, destroy the pages. Burn them or tear them up, but don't keep them.

This forgiveness strategy will help you clear away unresolved emotion and upset from the past that is draining you energetically. Time and time again, I have been privileged to witness people transform before my very eyes, privileged to witness them unburden themselves of the emotional baggage from the past that had been depleting them of their vitality and enthusiasm. To see them transformed with the help of this powerful tool of forgiveness is truly humbling and fulfilling.

Forgiveness brings peace within. Make peace with your past by sending sincere apologies to those who were at the receiving end of any wrongdoings you've committed. Forgive yourself and take any lessons from those experiences. Then draw a line through these events from your past. When you forgive yourself, you begin to foster a truer relationship with yourself, one based on trust in yourself, which nurtures ownership of situations. Your intuitive muscle is strengthened. You can become more reliant on your own intuition. All this culminates in self-growth. Forgive others, too, for the part they played in 'validating' a belief you had been holding. Sincerely, see their involvement as part of your 'learning' and forgive them for their involvement in you having this experience. Move on.

When you set future goals, give yourself permission to make mistakes, to get it wrong. When you get things wrong, you learn. This is actually a win-win. By allowing yourself to fail, you release any resistance and give yourself permission to proceed, which will ultimately lead to success. Allow others to make mistakes too, as it's through these that they learn.

Chapter 15

Our Superpower

"The way in which we think of ourselves has
everything to do with how our world sees
us and how we see ourselves successfully
acknowledged by the world."

Arlene Rankin

Every day we are exposed to a vast amount of information,
which we then filter. Firstly, through our senses, and then,
through mental filters in our minds. We have all experienced
seeing a painting or a beautiful view with friends, yet there will
be details that stand out to you and different aspects of it that
stand out to your friends. What you see is an interpretation
of the world. Your interpretation. Similarly, we can hear a
conversation and come away remembering a different version
of what was said than someone else who was also part of the
conversation.

Earlier, you saw how your early experiences, values,
influences by family, education and society can create
ambitions, expectations and beliefs about the world. These
filters will determine your approach and attitude to yourself,
other people and the world at large. Everyone has different
life experiences, beliefs and expectations. These make up the
roadmap of your world. Every single person has a different

mapping system for their world. Everyone thinks they are right, based on their own interpretation.

If you believe the world to be a cruel, dangerous place, your approach to life will be filtered through that belief. However, if your belief is that the world is an amazing place, full of opportunity and kind people, your thoughts, self-talk and life will be very different.

The great news is you can update your roadmap, alter your mapping system, *go deep* and operate through a different filter. When you *go deep,* you can get to the core and create an enhanced mapping system. *Going deep* into your consciousness allows you to truly transform, by bringing clarity and authenticity to your deep-rooted values, and your own purpose, which will bring profound changes in how you feel and how you communicate and behave.

To help you achieve this, you have a superpower. An amazing system that can, at your will, choose what information you focus on!

Everybody has within them something called the Reticular Activating System (RAS). This is located within your brain and is relatively small in size. Its functions are numerous and include the ability to consciously focus your attention on something in particular at a given time. The RAS is the portal through which almost all information enters your brain, except for your sense of smell, which goes directly into your brain's emotional area. Although we take in massive amounts of information subconsciously through our sensory organs, your RAS selects the ones that are important for your conscious mind.

Let me give you an idea of the quantity of information we are talking about here. Our conscious mind can process 40 fragments of information per second. However, our subconscious mind can handle *40 million* fragments of information per second. That's a lot! That's why I say your RAS is your superpower, because it filters out all the unimportant information that you don't need. This ensures you don't get overwhelmed, enabling you to focus on only important information.

Your RAS is your 'alert centre'. It takes instructions from your conscious mind, passes them to your subconscious mind, and acts upon your requests. There is a priority listing that your RAS adheres to. Certain details are instinctively alerted, such as your name and anything that threatens your survival, along with information you need immediately, like 'where is the nearest exit?', 'does this person seem safe?' or 'where is the nearest petrol station?'

This is part of the survival mechanism that responds to the beliefs we hold in our mapping. If we are using old roadmaps, you can see how this may be a problem. Your RAS uses your beliefs to create your reality. That's the good news and the not-so-good news! What if you are running a negative belief? Your RAS will constantly be seeking out information to validate that belief. If you have a belief that the world is a dangerous place, your RAS will focus on information it receives to prove itself right. It filters out unnecessary data and chooses data that is based on your outdated belief system. So, you can see how important it is to have thoughts that support you.

Let me give you a simple example of the RAS at work. I decided that I was going to change my car. I looked online to see which type of car would suit my family. A Renault Scenic caught my eye. And would you believe, the following day, I noticed so many Renault Scenics! Of course, there were always lots of Renault Scenics on the road, but now my RAS was tuned in to seek them out and bringing them to my attention.

If there is something you want to focus on, your RAS will be on the 'lookout' for that information from the data you are receiving through your senses. This filtering process goes on subconsciously, so you aren't even aware of it. Once you begin to program your RAS, it will work for you. It filters the world through the parameters you give it. We already spoke of how your beliefs shape your world. Now you understand how that is working, you have even more reason to *go deep* and clear out these old beliefs!

I remember when my children were younger, introducing new food into their diet would pose a challenge for them. Perhaps it was the fear of the unfamiliar. When I introduced something new, they viewed it with suspicion. Quickly, I learned to associate a sense of curiosity or fun with them trying new food. When making roasted tomato and pepper soup, I would throw in some sweetcorn; suddenly, the soup became pirate's treasure soup. The kids would then look for the treasure 'sweetcorn' at the bottom of the bowl. Butternut squash soup became 'happy soup' and spare ribs from the Chinese takeaway became dinosaur bones (Luca was nuts about dinosaurs). Many of the fun food titles we gave dishes have stuck over the years. In fact, recently, I accidentally ordered 'dinosaur bones' from our Chinese takeaway, much to the amusement of the staff member who took my order! With new experiences, we changed the children's perception from one of suspicion to fun and curiosity.

Your RAS can be your secret weapon, your superpower. It helps you see what you want to see and in doing so, influences your actions. How are you programming yours?

Chapter 16

It's in the Rehearsal

"Visualisation. It may be the most
important part of your mental package."

Ray Floyd

See It, Say It, Do It

When formulating your goal-setting strategy, consider this. When you see it, and say it, then follow up with action, you are more likely to achieve it. Napoleon Hill, author of *Think & Grow Rich*, put it quite succinctly: "What the mind can conceive and believe, it will achieve".

Following the examination of world class athletes, top level CEOs and the most accomplished artistic performers, researchers have found some common traits. They see it, they say it and they do it! These individuals visualise themselves achieving their objectives. Their internal self-talk is positive and motivating. With the seeing and saying comes the self-belief required to move forward. They can then take the required action to achieve their goals.

Visualisation is a simple yet powerful technique. It is a mental rehearsal of achieving your goals. It involves creating the ideal images, along with sounds and feelings, in your mind about a goal you wish to achieve. You picture yourself achieving your goal in the perfect environment, then replay this mental video repeatedly during the course of your day, every day!

Prior to 1954, doctors and scientists said that it was impossible to run one mile in a time less than four minutes. Many athletes attempted to break through this barrier. They all failed. On some level, they bought into the belief that it was impossible. Meanwhile, Roger Bannister, a junior doctor and Olympic athlete had set himself the goal of breaking that four-minute barrier. He could *see* himself being the first athlete to run a sub-four-minute mile. Even though his studies at medical school only afforded him one hour's training each day, he had the right self-talk. He believed he would be the first to do it. He knew it could be done. He trained at the Paddington Recreational Ground in Maida Vale, London from 1951 to 1954. On 6 May 1954, Roger Bannister ran the first sub-four-minute mile at Oxford University's Iffley Road Track. Roger Bannister didn't only break the four-minute mile barrier that day. He also broke the mental barrier that had held back so many athletes. He provided the belief that it was achievable. In fact, his record only stood for 46 days and has been broken by many athletes since then.

Another example that shows the effectiveness and success of using visualisation techniques was a study undertaken by Australian psychologist Alan Richardson. He took a group of basketball players, none of whom had ever practiced visualisation and divided them into three groups. He tested each player's ability to make free throws. He gave them the following instructions:

The first group practiced free throws every day for 20 days;

The second group practiced free throws on the first and last day;

*The third group also practiced free throws on the first and last day, **and** spent 20 minutes visualising their free throws every day.*

The results were astounding. The group who practiced every day had a 24% improvement rate. The group who practiced on the first and last day only had no change in their success rate.

The group who practiced on the first and last day, and spent 20 minutes each day using visualisation techniques had an improvement rate of 23%, almost an identical improvement rate to that of the first group. From just this study, it is evident that visualisation works!

The even better news is that anyone can use these visualisation techniques. It's a simple process, but it does, of course, require consistent practice. Here's what to do:

Fieldwork

Think of the goal or situation you want to achieve.

Take time to relax, away from noise and distractions.

Engage your imagination to create your mental movie of what you want to accomplish.

The more detail you use the better – see it, smell it, taste it, touch it, hear it, and lastly feel the emotions of achieving your desired outcome. Your subconscious mind takes in information through the senses, so include these in your visualisation. Napoleon Hill explains why connecting with those feelings is so important: "Plain, unemotional words do not influence the subconscious mind. You will get no appreciable results until you learn to reach your subconscious mind with thoughts or spoken words which have been well emotionalised with *belief*."

Once you have finished your visualisation, come back to the room and take a moment to bask in the glory of assuming the desired destiny.

Have no concern for the how.

Do not concern yourself with how this will happen, you are merely setting up the desired outcome, and then stepping out of your own way and allowing your subconscious to work out the details. Set the intention for what you want and let the universe work out how you will achieve your goal.

Make it a habit in your daily routine.

Spent 10 to 15 minutes on this activity, ideally twice during your day. Once in the morning and again before you go to bed.

Be in 'discovery' mode throughout the day.

Remember, you are training your RAS by instructing it what to focus on. Your RAS will seek the people, information and opportunities that will help you achieve your visualisation. Your RAS is influencing the world you see around you. Be on the look out for thoughts, ideas and feelings that bubble up, and take action. The more you listen and follow the clues, the quicker you will reach your desired goal.

When using visualisation techniques, the key is to create the mental movie of you already achieving your desire. Your RAS does not question the validity of the instruction. It *cannot distinguish between what is real and what is imagined*. It interprets and acts upon the predominating thoughts that are consistent within your conscious mind. Your RAS seeks circumstances and situations that validate your requests and beliefs.

Whatever your definition of success, you can achieve it. You can train your mind to think about what you want in life and make it happen. Keep your goals list active and updated. Take it with you wherever you go and re-read it often. In this way, you are continually reminding your brain of what is important to you.

Getting the Subconscious On Board

I remember when I was taking driving lessons. I had seen other people drive almost on autopilot and it looked so easy. However, I found it hard to remember all the key details. Now, I can sing along to a song on the radio, or think of my day ahead, while driving almost automatically.

We have all experienced the awkwardness of learning a new task or skill, like walking, or driving a new car, or even playing an instrument. It's clunky, robotic and amateur. Yet once it's learned and the subconscious takes over, we do it without thinking. Think of your last time you drove the car or walked to the shops. Were you 'aware' of the actions you needed to take? Changing gear, checking your mirror, or putting one foot in front of the other when walking?

We can see the benefits of sending clear specific instructions to our subconscious. This is the first part of achieving a desired outcome. It's the first part of *see it, say it, do it*. We need our self-talk and self-belief in alignment. We then need to take action, do what needs to be done to achieve the desired outcome.

Fieldwork:

In chapter 13 in the Parachutes section, we looked at the filing cabinet in your mind, which houses all your memories. It keeps a record of your negative experiences as well as your positive ones. In the following visualisation exercise, you can connect with a positive experience of the past in order to tap into that feeling for a particular event. Let's say you are going to a social gathering and you are feeling a little anxious about meeting people you may not know. Using that example, here's what you'd do.

When you think ahead to the event, what feeling would you like to have?

On this occasion, we want the feeling of confidence. The following technique is also available here **https://innergpssystem.com/confidence-technique/**

Find a quiet place away from distractions and noise. Put your feet on the floor and take a few deep breaths in.

Imagine a cord running down along your spine and reaching down into Mother Earth. Let this cord spread out like a root system into Mother Earth, accessing her bountiful treasures.

See a beautiful white light begin to make its way up from Mother Earth and up to the roots, travelling up the cord and up through your spine. See this pure white light effortlessly expand throughout your body, making its way up to your heart space. Here it gently spins your heart chakra. This is where your wonderful traits reside.

Think of a time when you felt confident and were enjoying being with other people. Connect to the feelings you felt and see yourself smiling. Connect to the lightness of the memory as you felt happy. Take a moment to really experience the feelings of this memory, of this energy, grateful for having felt it.

Imagine taking a morsel of this energy of gratitude and confidence and dropping it into the energy stream of this magnificent white light as it flows up from Mother Earth.

See the amazing white light continue up through your throat chakra and up to your crown chakra on the top of your head. From your crown chakra, this powerful white light exits your body as you offer it to the universe.

When anything is given in gratitude, it's returned a thousand-fold. See this morsel of energy now like tiny atomic particles of confidence and gratitude as it re-enters your body through your crown chakra. See it descend through your body.

Breathe in this feeling of confidence and gratitude. See this confidence and gratitude effortlessly expand throughout your whole body until it's completely filled.

When it fills your body, see this confidence and gratitude expanding out one foot around your body, like you *are* this confidence and gratitude. Feel yourself enveloped in this confidence and gratitude.

Notice how it feels and see how you look, as you smile confidently. See how you embrace your day from this confidence. Observe just how good it feels. Be aware how effortlessly you interact with other people, how light you feel and how much you enjoy other people's company.

See the whole event playing out and how much enjoyment you receive.

As you come back to the room, remain connected to this feeling. Keep breathing it in as you embrace your day. Reconnect again whenever you can.

Chapter 17

Simple, Repeatable and Positive

"You were designed for accomplishment, engineered for success, and endowed with the seeds of greatness."

Zig Ziglar

Now we've seen the 'see it' piece of the picture, let's look at the 'say it' part. In the last chapter, we saw how to visualise the desired goal and use an excellent technique that keeps the vision in our mental movie. Our inner self-talk can be our best supportive buddy or our worst annoying enemy. Keeping it as our best supportive buddy is a crucial next step to success.

Our thoughts are creative forces and are constantly echoing through our lives. Once we are aware of this, we can design our lives with clarity and purpose. When you verbalise something and repeat it to yourself, it influences your thoughts and how you speak to yourself on an ongoing basis.

For this, I find affirmations particularly useful. Affirmations work really well when it's for something that is not imminent, something that you are working towards longer term where the positive pep talk helps keep your mind chatter working positively towards that goal. Our RAS seeks out that which we focus on and affirmations help us focus on a desired outcome.

Affirmations can be said out loud or quietly to yourself. In my view, it's better to speak out loud your affirmation because you can add your own intonation and energy. As we know, your mind's subconscious is more likely to take in these instructions when they are interwoven with emotion and feeling.

There are a few aspects to bear in mind when you are creating affirmations.

Keep your affirmations positive in nature. Instead of saying, 'I don't want to mess up this interview', you could say, 'I will have a great interview'. It could be argued that both 'mean' the same; however, structure your affirmation so that it focuses on what you want to achieve instead of what you want to eliminate or avoid in your life

Use words that reflect what you want to have happen. Statements that contain words like 'might' and 'could' are not powerful statements, unlike statements that contain worlds like 'am' and 'do'. I find 'I am' statements most powerful. 'I am connected to my purpose' or 'I am positivity', for instance. Another good example, 'I speak confidently in interviews'.

Keep your affirmation short. They should be simple enough to repeat over and over.

Keep your affirmation in the present tense. Everything happens in the present moment. Your mind focuses on the present and doesn't communicate in future tense. Hence, when you are nervous about an event in the future, you feel that nervousness now. Your mind will not differentiate imagination from reality, so it processes the information literally and prepares for the action 'I am a confident employee' strengthens the neural connections that make you feel confident and determined and prepared for your interview.

Say your affirmation with the feelings and emotions that benefit your desired outcome.

When I use affirmations in support of my desired goals, I find just before I go asleep to be a great time to reaffirm what I want. Your conscious mind and your subconscious mind are most connected when you're sleeping. During those last few minutes of your day, you can set the intention of your affirmation and let it sit with your subconscious mind while you sleep.

Your mind is always looking for clues to filter your environment and guide your actions. If you don't have positive instructions for it to follow, it may pick up on the thoughts that occupy your mind. This could be the subconscious fears and doubts or judgements that you haven't dealt with. This is another good reason to keep your inner self-talk positive! Your mind is looking for instructions, so make them clear, specific and positive.

Repetition is a major factor contributing to the success of your affirmations. Your mind responds to present tense statements, but until it becomes an ingrained habit, you need to keep repeating these positive statements to yourself. Remember, it's like learning to drive. It's awkward at first, then soon you are driving on autopilot. You have to keep repeating this task until your brain strengthens its neuron connections. It's just part of learning anything. You consciously repeat the task, set up the neuron connections, until it's wired into your subconscious. Then the task of 'driving' (or whatever you are programming) will come naturally to you! If you don't drive and can't relate to this example, think of another activity you had to learn, a musical instrument perhaps. Anything can come naturally if you repeat it enough times.

You can create affirmations to assist you in achieving a desired outcome in all areas of your life. Here are a few you might like to use for everyday life. By repeating these affirmations a few times a day you will be amazed at how they can transform your everyday experiences:

Each day of my life is filled with joy and love.

I am enthusiastic about every second of my life.

I am a beacon of love and compassion.

All of my relationships are positive and filled with love and compassion.

I see others as good people who are trying their best.

Everywhere I look, I find opportunities to be kind and caring.

I easily accomplish all of my goals.

I have the power to create all the success and prosperity I desire

I embrace new avenues of income

My thoughts and feelings are nourishing.

I see beauty in everything.

People treat me with kindness and respect.

I am surrounded by peaceful people.

My environment is calm and supportive.

I am open and receptive to all the wealth life offers me

Money comes to me easily and effortlessly

My actions create constant prosperity

Chapter 18

Wow, Thank You!

"Life is not measured by the number of breaths we take, but by the moments that take our breath away."

Maya Angelou

When you look in the mirror, what do you see? Do you say, 'Oh wow, what an amazing person I am! What a wonderful face. Look at those features! I am a dazzling beauty'? Or do you look for the slightest blemish or flaw? When I look in the mirror, my eyes can be drawn to my many imperfections. Throughout the years, one set of blemishes has been swapped for another. The teenage acne is long gone, though crows' feet and grey roots are settling themselves in. Some we can mask with the help of a bottle of dye. Others, not so easily!

We can be our own worst critic, always finding fault with how we look, what we do or what we say. We are the very ones who know what we go through. Don't we deserve admiration, respect and love, especially from ourselves?

I started, some time ago, to take a moment each morning when I look in the mirror, to acknowledge that person staring back at me.

When you take a moment, when you really pause to look beyond the skin, when you stop to look deep into those eyes staring back at you and connect, you connect to her, you acknowledge her amazingness and you thank her for putting up with everything you throw at her. When you allow yourself to stop focusing on your imperfections and accept you for being you, when you acknowledge that you are more than your imperfections and start realising that you are beautiful, your RAS will be reprogrammed. You can then look in the mirror and see your qualities and a different version of you that perhaps you didn't notice before.

Acknowledging and accepting your own brilliance may not come too easy when you start actively doing this. Growing up in an Irish culture, we encourage modesty and avoid accepting compliments. When we begin to compliment ourselves, that's a strange feeling. For me, it was also emotional. When I looked long and hard at myself through soft eyes, my acceptance quickly resulted in seeking forgiveness from myself in the mirror. I carry out this mirror exercise for a few minutes every day and it does get easier. I have even come to like it. I like reminding myself of my good points. I thank the *me* in the mirror and that is powerful. Being grateful for yourself might sound a bit bizarre, but when was the last time you thanked yourself?

A phenomenon occurs when you do this. When you change how you view yourself, others take more notice too and their perception of you changes. Your outer world is a mirror of your inner world. When you change your inner world, the outer world will change to reflect it too. Thus, when you view yourself in a more positive light, as a beautiful, amazing person, and stop focusing on your imperfections, you will attract people into your life who see these positive traits too.

When you are grateful for something, the emotions that fill you are truly positive, and humbling. You can't be grateful and have a negative feeling at the same time.

Grateful Mirror Chat

A lovely way to start your day is to have your 'grateful mirror chat'. Take a moment during the day to remind yourself of other areas of your life that you are grateful for.

Extend that gratitude to your family. You could do this by quietly reminding yourself of the reasons you are grateful that they are in your life, or you can have a gratitude circle with everyone together. This is something I do regularly with my family. We began the practice of gratitude circles when one of the children was, yet again, finding fault with another. Humans can be quick to spot the negative, so as I heard my daughter Sadhbh give the reasons why her brother had upset her, I realised that it may be time for her to acknowledge something he had done for her. We sat around the kitchen table for our first gratitude circle and I gave them easy instructions. One person would be the focus as the other family members mentioned one nice thing that person did during the day. It can be the simplest thing. An example might be, "I am so grateful that you made me a lovely cup of coffee this morning", or "I am so grateful for the beautiful smile you gave me this morning". The first time we did this, they had to search for something to be grateful for, but they did find something. Each person loved being in the centre of the circle. Hearing nice comments and having their presence validated in such a positive and supportive way. Whenever we carry out this exercise, afterwards, there is always a calm atmosphere, where we are more loving and kind to one another.

Sometimes, it's just nice to be nice.

Chapter 19

A Moving Mantra!

"If you are successful, it is because somewhere, sometime, someone gave you a life or an idea that started you in the right direction. Remember also that you are indebted to life until you help some less fortunate person, just as you were helped."

Melinda Gates

One of the many motivational speakers that I listen to is Joe Vitale. I love his approach. One transformational tool he uses is called Ho'oponopono. Ho'oponopono is an excellent complement for all forms of self-improvement. The back story is fascinating. Here, I would like to give you a brief introduction to it.

'Ho'oponopono' is defined in the *Hawaiian Dictionary* as 'mental cleansing'. What is remarkable about Ho'oponopono is that it allows all participants to apologise, to forgive, and to move on with their lives in their community.

Hawaiian scholar Mary Kawena Pukui wrote, *"Ho'oponopono corrects, restores and maintains good relationships among family members."* Usually when there is an issue, the family is gathered and the most senior member of the family conducts this process.

The process begins by identifying the issue. This issue is talked over, then worked out and the matter is released. The feelings of everyone involved are discussed and acknowledged. Then by reciting the Ho'oponopono mantra continually, forgiveness takes place to the benefit of all involved.

In 1976, Morrnah Simeona adapted the traditional Ho'oponopono of family mutual forgiveness to the social realities of the modern day. She extended it both to a general problem-solving process outside the family and to a self-help process, for an individual. Whether you engage with this technique on your own or in a group setting, Ho'oponopono can transform your moment.

At the end of the last century, the courts in Hawaii began to order both juvenile and adult offenders to work with an 'elder' who would conduct Ho'oponopono for their families, as a form of Alternative Dispute Resolution.

After Morrnah Simeona's passing in 1992, her former student Dr. Ihaleakala Hew Len carried on her work. He worked in a psychiatric hospital for the criminally insane in Hawaii, an institution housing the toughest mentally disturbed criminals. The ward on which he worked was so challenging that the patients were usually shackled or heavily sedated. Staff who worked there often walked down the hall with their backs against the wall for fear of being attacked. Understandably, staff turnover was high. That's how dark this place was. That's how depressing it was. That's how scary it was.

Dr. Hew Len became famous, not for the miraculous healing of those criminals, but for the method he used. His approach was simple. Initially, he did not see any patients individually. He would sit in his office and focus on the criminal file of each patient. He would notice in himself the feelings, thoughts and judgments that arose as a result of what he was reading about each patient. Dr. Hew Len then used the Ho'oponopono technique and the behaviour of the patients began to improve. The patients started to get better.

Using Ho'oponopono can transform the moment.

When I meet someone for the first time, they appear in front of me with a clean sheet. I hold no data on them. I am in 'zero state' in relation to this person. Instantly, though, I start subconsciously writing on this clean sheet, making judgments and labelling the person as such and such a character. How the person looks, moves, talks, thinks and so on. I place my labels on this clean sheet in a matter of a few seconds of meeting someone new.

Even before we meet someone, we may have written on their clean sheet. I may discuss a person with a friend who knows him. I now have her judgments of him like, "Oh he is a lovely chap" or "I didn't warm to him!".

What if I heard he was an inmate in an institution for the criminally insane and is dangerous? When this person is in front of me, how might I react? How might he react to me with these judgments in place? Whenever he sees the judgment in my eyes, he will react accordingly... defensively. Even if he didn't behave according to the judgments I have in my mind, my reaction towards anything he is saying or doing will be interpreted according to my perceptions.

Check the image I have implanted in your head by saying "toughest mentally disturbed criminals in a mental institution". Add to that "restrained". I have provided you with the labels and prejudgment. How would you talk to or treat any of them if you happened to meet them? Is there any chance for that person to change or improve?

Before taking up his position at the hospital, Dr. Hew Len had only been made aware of cursory information about the patients. By using the Ho'oponopono cleansing technique, while focusing on each patient's file, he cleared out the negative feelings, prejudices and judgments that resonated inside himself. He did not apply the technique to anyone else, he applied it to himself, towards others. Remember, Dr. Hew Len had not yet met these patients. He was simply cleaning *himself* of any data that resonated with him about each of *them*, especially negative data. He did this in an effort to get to what he called "zero state". When he arrived at that, he felt no negative feelings towards them. In his own words, "I didn't care about them. I cared about myself. I wanted to clean myself. They have been brought into my life, and I need to clean this data from myself."

Clean himself from what? The reflection of his soul he is seeing in them.

Only when he reached that zero state did he start talking to them, without prejudice. And when he reached that zero state, the manner of those patients changed. This is the beautiful demonstration of something Mahatma Gandhi said, "Be the change you want to see in the world."

Let's take a look at the Ho'oponopono cleansing technique now. The mantra to repeat is as follows:

I am sorry – for whatever feeling you had-
Please forgive me - I love you - Thank you

Dr. Hew Len worked at that particular psychiatric hospital for four years. Within just a few short months of starting, people began to get better. They were less aggressive and less troublesome and required no sedation or shackles. The staff were happier working there and the patients were all transferred to less secure facilities.

This cleansing process involves four short sentences, repeated in whatever order feels right for you. Remember, you are directing these phrases towards your inner self:

I am sorry - Please forgive me - I love you - Thank you

By repeating these phrases, you are working on erasing negative knee-jerk reactions and clearing away your inner judgments.

Ho'oponopono is a cleansing technique that we can all benefit from as a regular practice. Whenever I feel a sense of judgment bubbling up inside me as a result of someone's behaviour, I take that as a cue to adopt the Ho'oponopono technique. After a few minutes, it transforms my moment.

Ho'oponopono can be used as part of a self-healing process, in the family or outside the family. The best part of the updated version of Ho'oponopono is you can do it yourself. You don't need anyone else to be there and you don't need anyone to hear you. You can say the words in your head even. Its power is in the feeling and the willingness of the universe to forgive and love. Try it for yourself... and let it transform your moment.

Chapter 20

Good Vibrations

"The energy of the mind is the essence of life."

Aristotle

We are gifted with energy each day. Depending on what we do during the course of those precious hours, this energy may increase, or it may decrease. Culturally, we are taught to conceal negative feelings and as a result we tend to suppress them. Suppressing our emotions can create heavy energy within us, some of which is used to 'maintain' old stories, the emotional baggage that you carry around with you.

By clearing the limiting beliefs, you are 'freeing' up this energy and will feel lighter energetically! If you have embraced and attempted some of the gentle exercises in this book, you may already be feeling their benefits. Your new interactions, thoughts and responses will have an incredibly positive effect on your ability to increase and keep your energy levels up.

The emotions of fear, guilt, shame and grief feel 'heavy', and can be found in the lower end of the emotional vibration scale. Anger, though often seen as negative, can lead to heightened levels of positive energy. It is the emotion associated with springtime; seeds need the energy of anger to push through the soil. Anger can often lead to great bursts of creativity. In the **Go Deep** section, I mentioned that anger likes action. If you are angry, you have fertile ground to be creative; the energy is on the move and you can propel it upwards towards the lighter emotional vibrations. When a client presents with anger, my response is - great, we can really get places with this!

When I studied Five Element Acupuncture, I was fascinated by the meridians throughout the body. Meridians are energy channels that are mapped across the entire body and facilitate the flow of energy through it. By tapping into these energy channels, you can effect an energy change. From time to time, these meridians can become blocked creating opportunities for a Five Element Acupuncturist to unblock your meridians and boost your energy level using acupuncture. I would always give patients a list of 'activities' that they could do to keep their energy vibration buoyant on their own too.

Beyond acupuncture to release the flow of stuck energy, the previous chapters have contained ideas to assist you in navigating towards your destination by clearing away the negativity and old stories. There are several other ways in which you can raise your vibration, lighten the mood and make your heart soar that I'd like to now share, because as you clear out negative emotions, you make way for more positive energy to come in.

Positive emotions include optimism, contentment, joy, happiness, love. Here are a few suggestions to help lift you up towards these high vibrations.

Reflect

What brings you joy? What makes your heart sing? For me, I love seeing the spring flowers popping out. Those courageous snowdrops and the first daffodils are a welcome sight. It's springtime, a time of planning, when the evenings start to stretch and the birds are singing away. It's hearing the children playing out on the streets again. These all make my heart dance. In the absence of springtime, there are other techniques I embrace in order to give my energy a lift and increase my good vibrations.

Music

I love listening to music when I am alone in the car. I can turn the volume up and sing out loud. Music speaks to my heart, to my soul. It helps me navigate at a higher vibration. At home, hearing a great beat will have us up on our feet as we dance with wild abandon. Thankfully, our children don't mind my two left feet, and usually join in with the energetic movements!

Meditation

I probably don't meditate in the conventional way. I've always found it a challenge to quieten my restless mind. My form of meditation, being in the moment and being mindful comes in the shape of cooking. I enjoy losing myself in the culinary exploration of a delicious meal for the whole family. I would happily spend hours preparing meals.

Nature

I am very much a 'fair weather' walker. Of course, the Irish weather doesn't help, although I do try to get out every now and then. Ambling along and just observing the countryside is a fabulous way of raising your energetic vibration. Taking a walk in a forest can supercharge those energy batteries, especially if you stay off the beaten track.

Gardening

Do you like to garden? There is something therapeutic about clearing out a space in the garden, sowing some seeds, and watching them flourish. They require very little from us, yet give so much back in return.

Water

I find something quite compelling about water. I could sit and listen to it for hours. Walking barefoot in a shallow stream or on a sandy beach can connect you to Mother Earth in a 'grounding' way. Leave the phones and office behind and take a tranquil walk along a river or the sea.

Socialising

Spending time with friends, unwinding, laughing, sharing stories and soaking up the love is top of my list for recharging your energy. We are hardwired for communication and connection with others. Surround yourself with friends and colleagues that are positive. Remember the effect our 'Radiators' have on our positivity, as mentioned in the Parachutes section? Endeavour to connect with these supportive people.

Take a note of activities that you like to do. Some activities, like singing, could be done in 15 minutes. A nice walk could be an hour and gardening might take a few hours. Write each activity on a piece of paper and put it into one of the following categories.

Category 1: takes 15 minutes

Category 2: takes an hour

Category 3: takes up to a few hours

Set aside three boxes and label them Category 1, Category 2 and Category 3.

Place all the activities in their respective boxes. Each day, randomly choose two activities from Category 1 or one activity from Category 2, depending on your time available. Each week, choose one activity from Category 3.

Take time out to raise your good vibrations!

Chapter 21

Uncovering Your Hidden Treasures

"I love the light for it shows me the way, yet I will endure the darkness because it shows me the stars."

Og Mandino

Look for the positives in the negatives with these questions... How can negative experiences move you towards your goals? In what ways can they help you thrive? What traits did you uncover about yourself as a result of certain negative events? I remember during one of my early *go deep* sessions, which was facilitated by my good friend Mary Hayes, I had to reflect on the benefits of my early childhood experiences. What traits did I now possess that I may not have had if I hadn't experienced these early events? Up until this point, I had only viewed these early experiences as negative. I had never been able to see these as anything else, let alone as having some kind of positive aspect. Although I would not welcome these events again, they did highlight some of my hidden treasures. What did I find?

Firstly, my resilience. I managed to make it through my childhood. I found strategies in the midst of a difficult situation to keep me safe.

Secondly, my instincts. My RAS was fine-tuned to detect subtle shifts in my father's moods. I was always on the lookout for danger. I returned home from school or from being out with my friends and would automatically slip into 'stealth mode'. I'd approach the house, usually from the back garden with a great degree of caution. Here, I could pick up on any shouting from within the house, which was frequent. I would peer in through the sitting room window and view that landscape. Were there any glasses or bottles of brandy on view? I would creep into the house, listening out for my father. If he was speaking to anyone else, I could quickly gauge his mood and take appropriate action. Sometimes that action was to turn on my heels and leave. I would then retreat to the safety of one of my *parachutes*, my Auntie Vera, who lived up the road.

Thirdly, my calmness and my empathy. My father wasn't angry with me all the time. There were times he would be fighting with the world as a whole or someone else would have upset him. There were times when I would be at home, safe, yet still having to contend with a drunk. I quickly learned strategies to calm and appease him. I would raise varying topics of conversation that tapped into his own lack of self-esteem and make him feel better about himself. As a consequence, I quickly learned to recognise the unspoken cries for help from others!

And there's more. Looking back at my childhood, I realise that I probably suffered from constant low-grade anxiety. Anxious people tend to be the best organisers. Anxious people think through and plan every possible step. They are alert to likely challenges ahead and have counter-strategies in place, should something go wrong. It's the swing of the pendulum, with anxiety at the dysfunctional side and organisation at the functional side.

My introverted ways may be attributable to my childhood experiences too, though I am not sure of this. However, I am certain that it made me a much better listener. While other people would be too busy trying to get their word in during a conversation, I would be listening. I'd listen to what wasn't being said or pick up on the emotion behind the words. I'd notice whether there was congruency between words and feelings or notice that there may be something more. This was something that came naturally to me. It is a trait that many of my clients have remarked on. My ability to see past their mask and really understand what they are all about. This skill was further enhanced following my near-death experience. I can easily see other people's outdated primitive roadmaps. I help them explore their hidden depths and uncover their true authentic selves in a sensitive and supportive way.

That my limiting beliefs were so mentally crippling to me brought many people into my life to shine a light on those. At the time, I viewed these people and situations as validations that I should remain small and in the background; that I *should* be invisible. Yet that screaming whisper was relentless.

I realised that situations and people enter into your life to help you *go deep*, to help you explore that which has been covered over. It becomes clear that there are rich learnings once you scratch beneath the surface of what is presented to you, and *go deep* into what is really there *for* you. I learned that life happens *for* you not *to* you. I have explored my inner depths and uncovered my true purpose. To speak to you, to share these words so as you too can explore what lies beneath your surface.

PART III

Explore Courageously

"Our deepest fear is not that we are inadequate. Our deepest fear is that we are powerful beyond measure. It is our light, not our darkness, that most frightens us. We ask ourselves, who am I to be brilliant, gorgeous, talented, fabulous? Actually, who are you not to be?... It is not just in some of us, it is in everyone. And as we let our own light shine, we unconsciously give other people permission to do the same. As we are liberated from our own fear, our presence automatically liberates others."

Marianne Williamson

Chapter 22

Change Your Narrative

"The way in which we think of ourselves has everything to do with how our world see us and how we see ourselves successfully acknowledged by the world."

Arlene Rankin

Throughout my life, my career path has been quite varied. Initially, career opportunities led me to working in Human Resources, where I developed invaluable organisational skills. However, the most interesting aspect of Human Resources was in fact the Human side of things. Working alongside people and assisting them with the various problems they encountered was the most fulfilling aspect for me. Looking back now to 1996, it seems an obvious progression that I began my studies in Five Element Acupuncture. This progression continued further as I added counselling and coaching to my skill set followed later by Journey Therapy and Radical Forgiveness. Indeed, I find myself continually *Exploring* new information, whether by immersing myself in a book or attending a course, constantly upskilling or adding to my coaching 'toolkit'. These skills have helped me develop my own *innerGPS*. It helped me reframe my past, unlock my potential and create the life I wanted. Now I hope it has helped you do the same. The *innerGPS* has been designed to help you step out of your shadow and allow you to follow a more authentic path. I hope you have found that path. Your path.

It was 10 January, 2006, when I was sitting at my computer, emailing some notes to a client I'd had a session with earlier that day. I heard that familiar ping, something new in my inbox. I opened the email, and as I read it, my heart sank. I could hear Fran playing with Luca in the next room, in stark contrast to the emotion I was feeling. Panic! I just sat there, not knowing what to do. It was two days later when I finally sat down with Fran and told him what was in that email. I had been asked by The Journey organisation to give a presentation on The Journey work in the region where I lived. They had organised the date for the presentation and needed someone adept at The Journey process to represent them. The date was set for 28 February at the Arklow Bay Hotel in Co. Wicklow.

Fran was silent for a few moments and then did something only a partner of a coach could do... He quoted me back to myself. He turned to me and said with a smirk, "So, what needs to happen for you to *stand out of your own shadow*?" Fran was right, of course, but it didn't mean I liked what he was saying. I had been encouraging clients to do it for years. Yet there I was, sick with the thought of stepping out of my shadow, stepping out of my perceived comfort zone and speaking to a large group of people that I didn't know. I remember saying to Fran, "I would rather die than have to stand up in front of a room full of people!"

Of course, it was a throw away statement. I didn't realise just how close to the bone those words would prove to be.

Over 100 people attended that presentation. I got through it and I received great feedback; however, I knew this was a skill I just didn't really have. I spent weeks fretting over this before feeling far too anxious to eat on the day of the presentation. Although I felt passionate about The Journey work, the anxiety was crippling.

Today, I thoroughly enjoy speaking to people. What changed? I have experienced several events that gave me the opportunity to take a good look at what was going on in my life. That evening I presented at the Arklow Bay Hotel back in 2006 helped me realise that, although I had been looking at some of my limiting beliefs, I was still working with my old roadmap. It was still in place. My new *innerGPS* needed regular 'upgrading'. This became abundantly clear after my near-death experience, later that same year. During my recovery, I was frequently visited with that screaming whisper: *'Be seen. Be heard.'*

I had a dilemma. I had already been immersed in therapy work and thoroughly enjoyed supporting clients in achieving their goals in life. However, after my near-death experience, I felt like a fraud. How could I call myself a coach if I had missed the learning in my own life? Why was I still running my 'invisibility' pattern up to the day of Callum's birth? Fran was studying homeopathy at the time and likened my situation to homeopathic treatment. He said, "Life is like the layers of an onion. We clear away one layer at a time, so as we have the awareness to move forward and clear another layer." I realised that I had just cleared some of my layers and others needed more work.

Life at home was busy with two young boys as my health slowly returned. During that first year after Callum's birth, I spend time peeling away more layers. As I've mentioned, that's when I undertook the work of Colin Tipping and qualified as a Radical Forgiveness coach. That night I spent in my father's hospital room, just prior to his passing, I felt such empathy for him. He was a man who was so misunderstood. He had never broken free from his primitive roadmap, yet he successfully ran an international club for penfriends, encouraging communication and understanding throughout the world. As I watched over him that night, I was overcome with sadness. He never got the opportunity to *go deep*, didn't have any *parachutes* in place, nor did he get the adequate support he required. He had no *strategies* for clearing out his old roadmap, with the result that his *innerGPS* was never activated. How different his life could have been if he did. My father couldn't change his narrative. However, I had an opportunity to change mine with this system.

Those visions that I saw during my near-death experience taunted me. I knew there was more I needed to do and I knew what it was. I needed to be physically seen and heard more. I needed to speak up! There! I said it!

I have a good friend Mohammed Al Hajeri, who told me about a public speaking group called Toastmasters and suggested I attend one of their meetings. Although I knew it would be a good fit for me, because Toastmasters is all about being seen and heard, I was not keen on the idea at first. For two years, I mentally switched off when he spoke about this group. At the same time, that little whisper got louder. *Be seen. Be heard.* Mohammed kept pushing me, until finally, in March 2013, I agreed to look into Toastmasters. I made enquiries and found out that their next meeting was that evening, and although my mind was very much against it, I thought I'd go along and see for myself what he had been talking about for the previous two years. Those old beliefs came screaming up, but I had my *innerGPS* in place and thought enough is enough. I needed to do this!

So I applied the *innerGPS*. The first step – *go deep* – revealed that my resistance to speaking in public was a deeply held belief that it was safer to be in the background, to be invisible. This belief was validated when I felt humiliated in school, the time I spoke out in front of the class. When I thought of speaking in public, I didn't think people would want to listen. Mohammed was one of my early 'public speaking' *parachutes*. I also used *strategies* of visualisation. I worked on my limiting belief and finally attended my first meeting.

This was when I met my second Toastmaster *parachute*, Colm Roe. From that first meeting, he was so supportive and put my mind at ease, offering me gentle encouragement. With the right *parachutes*, I could work on my skillset and my mindset. Mohammed and Colm became my unofficial mentors. These *parachutes* supported me, and when I lacked that inner positive belief, they guided me to where I needed to go. They gently supported me and encouraged me to give that first speech. I still recall it.

It was 2 July 2013, very soon after the passing of a wonderful man, one of my early *parachutes*, Mr. O'Byrne. I remember feeling extremely nervous, but also, strangely, I was amazed at how great it felt to be speaking in front of a group of people. A group that seemed interested in what I had to say. It was like the energy expanded. I could interact with so many people as I spoke from the top of the room. The feeling I had after giving this speech reminded me of when I did an actual parachute jump, back when I was 19 years old. It's that feeling of euphoria when you take on a challenge. It's facing your fears, pushing on through and conquering them. By making that first speech, I was fronting up to what I was scared of, and though I had a long way to go to conquer my fears, I was on the right road. With encouragement from Colm and Mohammed, I quickly signed up for my next speech.

There is something weird about willingly putting yourself in 'fearful' situations. Why would someone do such a thing? Maybe it's getting that adrenaline rush and the sheer thrill of accomplishing the goal. I was willingly putting myself in situations that brought on fear, but where was that fear coming from? My thoughts! And I knew that being heard and being seen were the exact opposite to a deeply held core negative belief I had. While I'd chipped away at it over the years, peeling back more layers and speaking in public was a large part of obliterating this core negative belief altogether. There was severe push back from my mind, of course. It was going nuts with my actions! It even tried, in a subconscious way, to sabotage those earlier speeches. I would get violently sick just before going to the meeting. My digestive system went into meltdown.

Yet I knew I was continually working on my *innerGPS*. I knew that the only thing holding me back were my thoughts. My *innerGPS* faced many challenges, yet I navigated them all, with the support of my *parachutes* and putting in place my *strategies*. I took action. I practised my speeches. I visualised myself enjoying sharing the information. Through affirmations, I gave myself pep talks. My inner self-talk became hugely supportive and I started *liking* public speaking.

As new members joined the club, my coaching experience helped them overcome their fears. I started sharing my *innerGPS* system with them. I embraced leadership roles within the club, and further afield within the organisation. My leadership *parachute* came in the guise of Brendan Haughton. He gave me the belief and support that I needed to meet several challenges I was facing. His unwavering faith in my capabilities gave me the strength to take on bigger challenges. Brendan was the ultimate cheerleader, though he was not a spectator. Brendan, when suggesting I take on bigger goals, was right beside me, supporting me all the way. One of those goals was to bring over the then World Champion of Public Speaking to Ireland. Nobody had ever been successful in getting a world champion to Ireland during their tenure as world champion. And this was unheard of at Division level, the level at which my leadership role resided. So, I contacted the then-champion, Mr. Mohammed Qahtani, and asked him if he would consider attending an event. He said, "Karen, you organise it, and I will be there." Mohammed is an amazing man who is so giving of his time. Although living in Saudi Arabia, he travelled to our events twice!

It was time to spread my wings. Supported by amazing *parachutes*, I plugged into training programs outside of the Toastmasters organisation and studied the World Class Speaking Program with Craig Valentine. This course has propelled me onto a variety of stages to speak and train. Another fellow speaker coach on that course, Bob Ferguson, has become one of my amazing *parachutes*. He is also my accountability buddy, and oh boy, does he hold me accountable, though in a lovely, gentle and supportive way. Thank you, Bob!

What has gotten me here, from where I was, is the regular upgrading of my *innerGPS*. Whenever fear, doubt or judgment creep in, that's my signal to *go deep*. I check in with my *parachutes* and I use the tools or *strategies* that I've put in place. And I take action. I am held accountable for my actions. Thankfully, I have a community of Explorers and we hold each other to account.

My father was a great writer of letters and had wanted to be a journalist. If times had been different, who knows, his wish may have been realised. I write this book in his honour, in honour of the man he could have been and the woman I became.

Today, I look back, not only with deep empathy for the little girl who went through those experiences, but also with admiration for what she went through. If it wasn't for the hardship and her determination, I would not be the woman I am today. I would not be able to be seen and heard. I would not be telling my story in the hope it inspires others to realise that they are not their story and they can change the narrative. They can drop the primitive roadmaps, tap into and enhance their own *innerGPS* and create a new destiny.

And you! You are your author. You decide what's on your next page, in your next chapter. So, change your narrative, my fellow Explorer!

Chapter 23

Step Out of Your Own Shadow

"It's only after you've stepped outside your comfort zone that you begin to change, grow, and transform."

Roy T. Bennett

People have asked me: When are you 'done' with *going deep*? When are you done with Exploring? My feeling is that for as long as you are travelling on this road of life, you will always need to update your *innerGPS*.

My journey thus far has taken me several years, many teachers, thousands of hours and several thousand euros. I have used a variety of tools and techniques. I have distilled the techniques that I have found transformational, into my *innerGPS*.

Wherever you are on your journey, check out your inner guidance. Does your mapping system require some tweaking? Invest in yourself *and* your future. Tune into what feels real and authentic for you. Engage your *parachutes* and ask for help. Create a community that supports your higher self. Above all, be kind to yourself and be patient. Upgrading your *innerGPS* is an ongoing process.

If you truly want to transform through a GPS system upgrade, I invite you to become an Explorer on my three-month program. You will be required to pop on your Explorers' lamp, shine it on those hidden depths and uncover your treasures. If you are committed to changing your narrative, navigating on your true course in life, come join our community of Explorers. During our expeditions, you will get reacquainted with the real you; you will deconstruct your old primitive roadmap of inner-core belief systems and install the upgraded *innerGPS*. You will *go deep* into untapped, undiscovered treasures with the assistance of fieldwork and reflective work.

You can design your new *innerGPS* with our Explorers' Workshop. This will provide *go deep* exercises, some *parachutes* and *strategies* for you to get on the right road to your ultimate destiny. This course is designed with your higher authentic self in mind.

Go check out **https://innergpssystem.com/explorers-insights/** and claim your *Free Explorer Insights* that accompany this book. This is my gift to you. A free *parachute* that will help you uncover your truth and reroute you with your *innerGPS*. This *innerGPS* video series can be used in a group setting, so you and your friends can be *parachutes* for one another as you journey together towards your true destinations. Sharing your victories with friends is a truly transformational experience. **Fly high, Explorers...**

Chapter 24

Explorers I met along the way

"Through relationships we grow and learn.
Through relationships we heal and are
returned to wholeness and truth. we need
others to mirror our misperceptions and our
projections and to help us bring repressed
material to consciousness for healing."

Colin Tipping

Jane's story:

"Everything that came from me came from deep deep within"

I have a bright light shining inside, a zest for life burning that cannot be suppressed, extinguished or dampened by even the darkest of winters. I did not always have this. A journey of sorts has taken me to this place within me, a place where anything and everything is possible. I am happy in my heart, happy in my head, happy in my soul and spirit.

I spent a very large part of my life in an unreachable place. From an early age I became invisible, a fantastic superhero power. I did not run with the pack, I ran with the underdog, I followed no one, independent, very sensitive to the world and all of its problems. People's feelings of anger, rage, hurt, pain, small glimpses of happiness consumed and strangled me. I wanted to heal the world, feed the starving children, save my mum and siblings from the physical and emotional abuse they had to endure. I became somewhat of an empath unknown to myself.

I developed a lot of amazing belief systems as a kid that were indeed beneficial up to a certain point in my life. Unknown to me at the time, I managed to carry them through into my adult life where they severely hindered my emotional, physical and spiritual growth. From disordered eating to other self-destructive behaviours, the constant monkey chatter in my head, berating me and putting me down. My hamster wheel which I never stepped off for fear of the past catching up with me and a torrent of emotions and feelings that would drown me if I stopped. It petrified me. All of it.

The tunnels were getting longer and darker and the glimmer of light at the end grew more faint, smaller and unreachable. I was falling harder and for longer and nobody could reach me. I would retract from society, friends and family while I tried to surface from a jerky hole, just falling, trying to catch or hold onto something that would light my way back to a socially acceptable normality. I did not want to live this life anymore. I needed someone to help me.

My very first session with Karen, was very much a wow moment for me. There were tears, anger, joy, so many emotions that just needed to find a way out. I can only describe it as earth shattering and a tremendous leap into the unknown. The approach is one that I had never come across before. Everything that came from me came from deep deep within. Karen created an environment and a safety net that felt true and real. I wanted to understand all the belief systems that were surfacing and so badly wanted to move forwards or "onwards and upwards" which became our mutual philosophy. The peeling of layers, sitting with and accepting emotions and feelings rather than running from them. A very new concept for me at the time.

Karen was by my side through all. There was a flow of emotions both painful and otherwise just bursting to be heard. I reconnected with me in a very different way. It may sound strange but reconnecting with my inner child was the key for me. This is where and when all my former belief systems originated and held true. This is something I had to do in order to move forward.

No medication, no being led in directions that made no sense. It was all me. Just peeling off the layers, patience and a mega jigsaw puzzle. Although Karen may have seen the result long before I did, she never revealed it. I made or rather created this jigsaw puzzle from start to finish and the feeling of seeing all the pieces fit into place is perhaps or was perhaps one of the most defining moments in my life.

Karen facilitated my return to ME and gave me the tools I needed to move forward. To say that, it is truly not enough. She is my "Earth Angel" and will forever be so. For the skills she presented me with have redefined my life. I may not be in a job that is challenging but it is fulfilling. My work is my playground, my life is far more. I have found love, a life filled with what if's and here afters. I have never felt so content and happy.

One of the first questions I was presented with when I initially met Karen was " what do you hope to gain from this session"? My reply was simple, a quiet mind, to feel happiness, contentment, to be a part of life, no more darkness. I achieved this and far more.

Thank you to my "Earth Angel"

Jane, Meath

Michael's story:

"I got to the heart of my main issue and the story and emotions behind it"

When I began working with Karen, I had just completed 3 years of counselling following the breakdown of my marriage. The counselling had opened my eyes to so much that I was unaware of about myself, other people and their behaviours and about life in general. I knew that I wanted to continue to explore all these areas further.

I knew that whilst counselling had been extremely beneficial in discovering and understanding myself, it didn't necessarily mean that the emotions and behaviours underpinning how I dealt with my issues had been removed.

Initially, I went searching on the internet for some EFT practitioners, but I was limited in my options and having come across the story of Brandon Bays and her Journey Process, I also searched on practitioners of her work. Karen was the only person to respond and the way she did made it clear to me, even without speaking with her, that she was the person to work with.

Having spoken on the phone and arranged an appointment I travelled down to her house just outside Tinahely, Co. Wicklow. The experience was life changing. It was the first time that I had ever experienced working with an 'alternative' therapist (I am not sure why we need to refer to it as alternative given that it is far more empathic and natural than 'conventional' therapies). During that initial session, I got to the heart of my main issue and the story and emotions behind it, followed by the release of those emotions and the forgiveness and understanding that followed.

It was exhausting and challenging, and the crying and blubbering were not a pretty sight but all through the process, Karen's gentle, firm and supportive guidance created such a safe and encouraging space.

That night, I slept for 16 or 17 hours and I felt significantly lighter in myself. It was the start of my own journey and deep dive into the world of personal change, energy work and broadly speaking, into the spiritual side of life which up to that point had not been of interest to me.

I had another session with Karen a few weeks later which again was profound, and I have attended further sessions with her in the intervening years. I have also recommended friends to her and her work and I know that their experiences were remarkable too.

For me, Karen is a wonderful person, extremely kind but also thoroughly professional in her approach to and delivery of her therapeutic work. I cannot recommend her highly enough.

Michael, Wexford

Lucy's story:

"As I focused on seeing my mum as an actual person underneath all the negativity our relationship changed for the better"

One of the best things about working with Karen was having someone say what I was thinking but afraid to utter. She made me see that it was ok to be myself and it has served me well in the years following our sessions. She was honest and kind and I found this very empowering.

Initially, we worked through some of my abandonment issues from my childhood. I had no idea that they were still affecting me 35 years later or in fact, that I even felt abandoned. We did some deep work where I came to some understandings about why they went away so often. I also discovered confusion from the fact that I understood that they loved me but were still leaving me with friends on a regular basis while they travelled.

What I had not realised until this point was how much this was affecting my relationship with my son. He was about 13 and we had only spent about two nights apart. I did not leave him with anyone. Until I looked into my beliefs with Karen, I had no issue with this but once I saw that the behaviour came directly from my own childhood, I was able to loosen the ties and realise I could be a good parent even if I went away without him overnight. I believe this has helped enormously as he has grown to be a self-sufficient, travelling adult. Karen was amazing throughout this process and I was not at all self-conscious about talking to her honestly.

I was also struggling with my relationship with my mother. When we started coaching sessions my father was very sick. After he passed away, my interactions with my mother became more and more draining. By working through this with Karen, I began to understand where my mother's actions were coming from. Over the course of a few sessions, I began to see that Mum is fearful of the unknown and new situations. I was full of judgement for her. This was not helped by the fact that we were both grieving for my father. I came to see that a very small percentage of our stressful interactions were in relation to what was currently going on and the rest was all the stories I was telling myself from the past. This made it much easier to let it go.

As time passed, I found some new understanding for Mum, but I was still struggling with her negativity. Karen gave me techniques to assist me. These were life changing. As I focused on seeing my mum as an actual person underneath all the negativity our relationship changed for the better.

It was honestly a life saver to have Karen to talk to and give me feedback throughout all these years.

Lucy, Dublin

Joan's story:

"I had buried it so deep, put a lid on it and now it was taking its toll"

I was stuck emotionally, just surviving knowing in my heart I needed help. Once I made that decision, that I needed help, it's amazing how the right person comes to you, to start the journey of healing.

For me it was Karen, a lady of kindness, support and wisdom. I was given my time, nothing fazes her.

After my first session I came away feeling powerful, in a very good headspace, physically flexible and light in my body.

Together we worked on all the layers, as they came up. What became very evident was the abuse and anger I was holding onto, from events that happened in my childhood. I had buried it so deep, put a lid on it and now it was taking its toll. I was unable to have a loving relationship with myself. Having carried around this emotional baggage, it had affected every area of my life. It took a lot of my energy to just keep a lid on it and I was emotionally exhausted. Once I accessed these buried memories, I cleared away the hurt and pain, with Karen's guidance, help and support. She provided a safe space of comfort, where I could regain my confidence and self-worth. These sessions involved 'going deep' process work, which resulted in some tears and also lots of laughs and 'aha' moments. I always left the sessions feeling more empowered.

I have made in-roads and progress, having a better relationship with all, especially myself. I now have the tools to continue making progress and I continue to allow the Universe to guide me on this journey that started with Karen. Thank you.

In love and light,

Joan, Kildare

Khalid's story:

"Karen's style of questioning creates a deep awareness within"

Regardless of the big number of self-development presentations, trainings and workshops I attended, in time of crisis I forgot all of this and felt down, depressed and hibernated in my own imaginary cave. Being depressed in my cave is something that I didn't want anyone to disturb. I was enjoying watching the world through my cave opening as if nothing mattered to me.

It was a work colleague who suggested Karen as a coach. Being coached, remotely over this long distance was not an idea that I thought would work, however, after our first Skype session, with Karen, I signed up for her 6-month program. Karen knows how to make you talk while she listens carefully and directs the conversation so as you find the solution yourself. She is always in the best friend's seat in your life. Karen's style of questioning uncovers a deep understanding of you, the client. She gets to know you deeply in order to effectively coach you without feeling it. She watches your progress carefully and patiently and gently pushes you forward and follows up with your progress. Karen's style of questioning creates a deep awareness within. A way for you to see what is truly happening in your life. From this perspective, it's easy to make the right decision. Karen helped me uncover my own potential and magnify my strengths whilst working on improving my weak areas for my benefit.

With Karen, I never felt like hiring a coach, but I felt like having a best friend. All my doubts about distance coaching evaporated with the progress I made with Karen.

With Karen, it is not the business that is driving her but the passion. She so much takes the coaching as a responsibility. She goes the extra mile and supports clients professionally on personal levels.

Coaching can greatly enhance your personal life though also helps you create a super power for your business!

Khalid, Saudi Arabia

Audrey's story:

"After each session with Karen, I can only describe it like swimming in a beautiful lake and coming out completely free and cleansed. I was ready to take on the world!"

Karen and I go back such a long way over school years both in primary and secondary.

We hooked up again through Facebook over at least 10 years ago and we rekindled our friendship but what I learnt about Karen over the past 10 years is she is more than a normal friend. Karen is the type of person that you could call on anytime of day and night to ask for help. She is a rarity in this modern world where people only fit you into their time when they are free instead of making time to free up for you.

Back in 2010 I went through a marriage separation from a man I was married to for 14 years. Through the year of 2010 to 2011, I sincerely was emotionally drained and felt I was truly on some spiral of a mental breakdown and though I was never diagnosed clinically with depression I was seriously depressed.

This is where Karen stepped in. She saw my sadness and spoke to me about her line of work and that it involved mindfulness, coaching, mentoring etc. I was a tad reluctant to open my heart to her as being school buddies I thought it was a bit too close to the bone. How wrong was I !!

She helped me to reframe my past and to work towards the future, to drop the guilt and focus on what makes me happy as a mother and a person. Karen and myself spoke at length of undoing the blueprint that I had marked as gospel for my life, to set myself free and let go of any guilt for wanting to be happy. Karen shared many tools and techniques with me. We wrote down all my good qualities which to be honest is a really hard thing to do as not many of us know or can admit our good qualities as it is seen as vain. We are so quick to believe the bad stuff about ourselves. She always made me laugh, telling me to say I was Zena the Mighty Warrior, but you know what, some days it worked.

Karen taught me to be happy in my own skin, to embrace every single day, to take the bad days with a pinch of salt and know that they are part of the journey.

The sessions I spent with Karen have remained valuable lessons, which I incorporate into my daily life now. She taught me how to respond to a crisis rather than react. She instilled in me that I was a warrior and could take on anything once I believed I could. Karen showed me to clear all hidden limitations. She taught me that it is ok to say No and to be assertive again. I had lost all of this on the way trying to people please. I have learnt to stand up for myself. Karen reminded me to accept myself and to accept my decisions in life; to learn to forgive myself and each time a negative thought came into my mind that I was to imagine a big STOP sign and get back on track. Karen gave me back my self-worth and reminded me that my children loved me and that I deserved to be happy.

After each session with Karen, I can only describe it like swimming in a beautiful lake and coming out completely free and cleansed. I was ready to take on the world!

Karen taught me to feel positive, confident and remember that anything is possible. I got back my confidence and I manage my mind much better now.

I truly feel that I would never have gotten through 2010 if Karen didn't have my back. Karen was so much of a friend/mentor/life coach that when my final court hearing for divorce came through that she drove me in court and sat coaching me through this horrific ordeal.

Everyone should have a Karen O'Donnell in their life !

My lovely Dad died tragically this year after a very short-lived illness. He was my hero and I adored him so much. He told me during my divorce that I was truly the strongest person he'd ever encountered. Though I am grieving exceptionally more so than I ever dreamt of, I truly believe that without my sessions with Karen *back in 2010/2011 I would never be fit or able to deal with the huge void my Dad has left behind. Karen gave me the skills to embrace life and enjoy all the happiness I can get.*

Audrey, Dublin

Vicki's story:

"Throughout our sessions, each of the issues was treated empathetically"

I went to Karen on recommendation from a friend. Prior to my first appointment with Karen, I had tried various treatments for panic attacks. Although I knew nothing really about panic attacks, I felt I was not the typical type of person to get one.

I was about 33 when the first panic attack happened, and it went on fairly regularly for the about 8 years. I became a prisoner to panic attacks. I was a shadow of my former self – the once independent, confident person was long gone.

I had tried lots of therapies to help understand the panic attacks. Whilst I learnt to understand the causes on some level it didn't really stop them. I still felt like a prisoner when I was 43.

By the time I met Karen, I'd had enough. I was at the end of my tether. I had tried lots of therapies, but nothing seemed to help the panic attacks and anxiety go away. Karen was fabulous. From the get-go, I trusted her. With all the stuff that went on in my life that I was ashamed of, felt guilty about or felt I couldn't say the words out loud cause that would have meant they were true, she didn't judge. She listened and did her stuff. Throughout our sessions, each of the issues was treated empathetically. I felt I was for the first time being true to me. I was acknowledging the stuff that went on in my life that I had swept under the carpet – too embarrassed, too ashamed.

Karen and I worked through these issues sensitively, chipping away the emotional hurt. Freeing myself from the past. Although it was hard work emotionally, it was liberating. Some people advised me just to take a tablet. Whilst this might have calmed me down, it would never got to the source of the problem. It is hard work facing deep emotional hurt. Plenty of tears along the way but my I have always said 'better out, than in'.

Painful and emotional as it was, I really enjoyed my sessions with Karen. As well as clearing the past, I learnt so much about human behaviour, how the mind works and learning that putting myself first, is not selfish. When I finished my journey with Karen, I really missed our sessions. But I knew it was time to move on; to live my life free from the past.

Vicki, Wicklow

Jean's story:

"We touched on deeply painful stuff and yet by the end of it, I felt calm and empowered"

In 2013 I was diagnosed with breast cancer. This came as a great shock to me. I became extremely fearful and anxious. I used some conventional treatment and embraced a naturopathic approach using a combination of diet, juicing, exercise and personal inquiry.

I realised that I needed to change the way I was leading my life. I felt "empty" inside. Felt no joy and thought "is this all there is to life". Help was needed and I had heard about Brandon Bays "Journey Work". I searched online and found several therapists doing this work. Karen O'Donnell was one of them. I spoke to Karen on the phone and intuitively, she felt like the right choice for me.

However, on my first visit to Karen, as she was guiding me with visualisation, I found myself thinking "What does she know? I've done this type of thing before. She is far too young"!!! I wanted to stop and walk out.

I quickly assessed the situation I was in! My back was to the wall. I needed to deal with emotional trauma and blockages that may have contributed to my cancer diagnosis. I wanted to heal and if I walked away now then what!?

So, I made the decision to stay for the session and give it a chance.

It was one of the best decisions I made in my life. That first session was powerful. We touched on deeply painful stuff and yet by the end of it, I felt calm and empowered.

She may be young, but she is very wise!!!

The process of 'going deep' involved closing my eyes and with Karen's guidance, imagining myself going down through the centre of my body, down through the layers. This was very hard to do in the beginning. I had to learn to trust what I felt or saw. Karen was very much with me as I described the images or feelings. It was as if she was there too.

Along the way she made suggestions or asked a question. This helped me to engage deeper, be curious and allow the feelings and images to emerge. My inner self felt heard and supported. I felt safe. This allowed me to become aware of the emotional pain, the sadness, the guilt, the shame and the negative beliefs I carried about myself!! Near the end of each session, Karen guided me towards what was called the "campfire". Here I gathered people around the campfire, particularly those whom I felt hurt by and I talked to them about how I felt hurt or whatever. There, the acknowledgement, forgiveness, healing and opening of my heart occurred. After these 'Go Deep' sessions, I felt feelings of love and joy.

I continued to work with Karen for over four years. I presented with all kinds of feelings e.g. disempowerment, terror, fear, vulnerability, anger, shame.

We went very deep to painful places and through her skillful, insightful, intuitive, kind and compassionate enquiry with me, I came away from these sessions feeling calmer, more centered, stronger, happier and lighter.

She provided the nurturing space for me to go deep, go beneath the terror and find my strength, my calm place, my deeper self.

It is now 2 years since I worked with Karen. I honestly do not know how I would have coped without her support. Life is very different for me now. I no longer feel "empty". I feel full of love and appreciation.

Of course, there are times when I don't feel the "love", when I am aware of challenges. The difference now is that I have a valuable tool which is ...to pause and take the time... to "Go Deep" and look within.

Do I wonder "is this all there is?" No, because it's not "out there". It's within. It's Love.

I highly recommend Karen. She is gifted, insightful and wise. I trust her and it's wonderful to be with someone who does not judge you no matter what. She is a joy to work with and I love her sense of humour.

Jean, Tipperary

Bill's story:

"I really liked Karen's ability to understand the challenges I faced and to some extent the pain, sense of shame possibly isolation that was causing my fears"

I approached Karen O'Donnell because she was a long-time acquaintance and she knew the theatre in which I was operating in for so many years.

I was in my mid-fifties, living alone in Middle East and operating as a lone wolf in my company. The symptoms I had at that moment was that of palpitations, unworthiness and found, for example, that shopping malls and airport queues became too much to handle.

Karen O'Donnell helped me by, introducing me to this innerGPS concept and slowly bringing me round to travelling back to Ireland and getting together for the first session.

At the very end she played a song, 'I forgive you, Me' by Karen Taylor-Good, which to this day still stimulates me and I have listened to this on numerous occasions since I first heard it. This was a fantastic way to finish off the session.

I really liked Karen's ability to understand the challenges I faced and to some extent the pain, sense of shame possibly isolation that was causing my fears. In a way she became my cheerleader with encouragement and very positive support. Guiding me in the right direction and allowing me to make good decisions going forward and to help me work through this depression or anxiety that was affecting my ability to function on a social basis. She also introduced the skill of breathing properly and the immediate benefits of doing so and by breathing in and out to relieve the stress, tension and blockages within the inner me.

Bill, UAE

Exploring Resources

Join the Explorers Book Club

https://innergpssystem.com/explorers-book-club/
and get access to:

- Explorers guide to clearing roadblocks

- Monthly online 'check ins' with Karen

- innerGPS tips on success, mental clarity and happiness

Further Reading

The Journey, Brandan Bays

Radical Forgiveness, Colin Tipping

See you at the Top, Zig Ziglar

The Gift of Acabar, Og Mandino

Move Ahead with Possibility Thinking, Robert Shuller

Getting the Love you Want, Harville Hendrix

I Need Your Love – Is it True?, Byron Katie

Dare to Lead, Brené Brown

Even Eagles Need a Push, David McNally

Think & Grow Rich, Napoleon Hill

Fierce Conversations, Susan Scott

What to Say When you Talk to Yourself, Shad Helmstetter

Feel the Fear and Do it Anyway, Susan Jeffers

The Road Less Travelled, M. Scott Peck

Lean In, Sandy Sandberg

Abundance Now, Lisa Nichols

Celestine Prophesy, James Redfield

The Four Agreements, Don Miguel Ruiz

The Power of Positive Thinking, Norman Vincent Peale

How to Win Friends & Influence People, Dale Carnegie

The Monk Who Sold His Ferrari, Robin S. Sharma

The Power of Words, Mohammed Qahtani

World Class Speaking, Craig Valentine & Mitch Meyerson

About The Author

Karen O'Donnell, creator of innerGPS, helps people find their purpose and live the life they truly deserve. A former European HR Officer for a Middle Eastern company, Karen diversified her work and followed her interest in personal development and emotional intelligence. Karen's Transformational Coaching programs incorporated her background in HR as well as over a decade of training in a variety of counselling and coaching modalities.

She assists clients in uncovering and clearing out 'limiting belief' roadblocks that are encountered along life's journey and has a keen passion for people stepping out of their own shadow and empowering them to live the life they were born to lead.

Karen is also an award-winning speaker and has merged her coaching skills with public speaking to bring interactive sessions to groups in a various communities, including the Dóchas Centre women's prison and students in primary, secondary and tertiary education.

Karen has also brought her innerGPS programs to teams in corporate settings. Karen's presentations all embrace the heart-centred themes of emotional intelligence and connection, which forms the basis of this innerGPS system. She also conducts presentation skills workshops to assist people in stepping out of their own shadow and being heard, through public speaking.

Karen has been featured in several publications in print and online, such as: Network She, *Top Consultant*, *Western Morning News*, *Western Daily Press*, Family Friendly Working website, *Empowered Business* magazine, *The HR Director*, *Entrepreneur & Investor* and *Executive Secretary*. She has also spoken professionally at Galway Ten Ten Talks, and internationally at Toastmasters International.

Karen helps clients navigate the roadblocks in life, assisting them in finding their voice and changing their narrative, so that they can live the life they were destined to live. Karen is in the business of possibilities, of assisting you in materialising your goals through the innerGPS system.

Karen runs her thriving business from her home in Wicklow where she lives with her husband and three children. And remember her wish to have a third child? In 2008, her daughter Sadhbh was born; a constant reminder of our own inner light, she always seeks to be heard and seen!

Connect with Karen

Join the Explorers book club:
https://innergpssystem.com/explorers-book-club/

Gain support by joining our Facebook community:
https://www.facebook.com/groups/innerGPSexplorers

Email Karen at:
connect@innerGPSsystem.com

Follow Karen on Twitter:
@Karen_speaker

Connect with Karen on Linkedin:
https://www.linkedin.com/in karenodonnellpublicspeaking/

Acknowledgements

Writing my first book was like being on a roller coaster ride... Lots of ups and a few downs. Some frustrating times and some very exciting times. The beauty of writing a book, although the actual writing of it is a solitary activity, most of the rest of the book's development has been a process involving several amazing people. They gave of their time so selflessly, people who brought their expertise and suggestions whole heartedly, resulting in this book you have before you - the sum total of their amazing contributions.

Everyone listed here has influenced this book's development in some way. My sincere thanks, to each and every one of you.

My family

My parents always spoke of possibilities, and were always open to my various ideas over the years. My mum Carmel, who cheered me on, on this whole writers journey. For a few years she has heard me talk of writing this book and when I finally put 'pen to paper' she encouraged me and listened to various extracts from the book. She had uncanny insights, a truly amazing woman. Thank you Mam for always supporting my ideas. My brother Liam and my sisters Nikki and Sharon who are never far from offering their helpful suggestions.

My husband Fran, for originally suggesting I write this book. Has endured several nights of reading early drafts, doing mock ups of book covers and providing many a cup of needed coffee as I burned the midnight oil in writing this book. Fran you have been a tower of strength, thank you. To my children, Luca, Callum & Sadhbh, you kept it real, gave me your honest feedback on various passages and offered words of encouragement and support. My heart overflows with love for you, as I watch you grow into 3 amazing explorers.

My wonderfully perceptive Aunty Vera, one of my early parachutes in life and also an early reader of this book. Gave me her heartfelt feedback and support. Thank you.

Uncle Bobby whose daily phone messages would spur me on. Your enthusiasm each morning was refreshing and always brought a smile to my face.

My friends

I am blessed with amazing friends both near and far. Their gentle words of encouragement always came along when I was unsure of my next step forward. A kind word here and there was enough to keep me moving forward.

My early readers – the thoughtfulness and considered attention to my book was invaluable. I am bowled over with your generosity and kindness in reading those early copies. Mary Butler, Eva McKenna, Dr. Frank McKenna, Colm Roe, Bob Ferguson, John Doyle, Brendan Haughton and Gerry French, a thousand thanks.

A special thanks to Caterina Rando who set up the Get Your Book Done NOW Facebook Challenge – you were so encouraging and offered those amazing writers' rooms where we didn't feel like we were writing in isolation.

My fellow journey therapists and long-time friends, Mary Hayes and Adrienne Small. Thank you for the cosy chats and keeping it real for me.

My Toastmasters family, especially the members of Dublin 18 Toastmasters. Thank you for your feedback on my speeches around innerGPS. My buddies at the Professional Speakers Association – always on hand to offer advice and feedback. 'We can and we will', Amanda and her group along with my facebook friends near and far, who gave so willingly of their time to comment and give their feedback on logos, book covers and titles.

Kapil Khanna for your time, encouragement and expertise, in helping me clarify my vision for my book and beyond.

My Editor Kris Emery – who lovingly edited my manuscript and looked after my work as if it was her own. Your talent as an editor is quite extraordinary – thank you for your attention to detail.

Everyone at YouCaxton Publishing – you expertly walked me through the whole publishing process and brought my book to life.

Thank you to the innerGPS expedition team who selflessly brought news of this book to places I couldn't reach on my own. You have helped me share this innerGPS system with fellow 'life' explorers. I have listed these amazing people on the following page.

I would also like to thank those fellow explorers who trusted me to be their guide along their journey back to themselves. Your whole-hearted courage is truly inspirational. You trusted my guidance when you would *'go deep'*. I was very humbled that you chose me to parachute in and be your guide. You consciously embraced the strategies, and continue to live the life you want to live.

For my readers, I acknowledge your readiness to step out of your own shadows and explore the life that's there for you.

Onwards and upwards fellow explorers.

innerGPS Expedition Team

Andrew Dobbin
Asumpta Gallagher
Michelle Johnston
Denise Fay
Lefford Fate
Aoife O'Brien
Orlagh Murphy
Phillip O'Brien
Pat Green
Niamh O'Meara
Gerry French
AnneMarie Graham
Shane Phelan
James Gargan
Teri Morris
Rachel Davies
Yasmin Vorajee
Deborah Cipollina
Declan Garvey
Vinette Hoffman-Jackson
Theresa Devine
Aoife Hayes
Gillian Keogh
Martin Blake
Maire Garvey
Adrienne Doyle
Kaylene Ledgar
Aoife Gaffney
Karen Broderick
Helena Tubridy
Danny Riley
Liz Valloor
Mary Fletcher-Burke
Kapil Khanna
John Dunleavy
Aklil Webb
Taha Boksmati
Keith Bradley
Johann Callaghan
Niall Cosgrave
Sharon Rossignuolo
Lottie Hearn
William Cotter
Orla McEvoy
Raluca Erimescu
Brendan Haughton
Martina Shaw
Mohammed Qahtani
Alan Murray
Baya Salmon-Hawk
Eamonn O'Brien
Steve Callas
Emily Gallagher
Edmond Carroll
Bob Ferguson
Niamh McCarthy
Maria McHugh.

BV - #0009 - 230819 - C0 - 229/152/11 - PB - 9781912419906